Ron's Investment Philosophy for Wealth

Mastering Time & Money to Join the Top 2%!

By
Ron Weber

This publication is designed to provide expert and useful information regarding the subject matter covered. Laws and practices vary from country to country and state to state. If legal or other expert assistance is required, the services of a professional should be sought. It is important to understand the following disclosures:

- Investing entails risk, including the risk of loss of principal.

- The materials presented are for informational purposes only and are not intended as a recommendation or advice designed to meet the needs of any specific person.

- You should not act on this information without first discussing your investment objectives with a financial professional.

- Price volatility and unrealized losses for equity investments can be significant, especially over shorter periods of time.

- While not a guarantee, achieving the potential benefits of a long-term, equity-investment strategy requires the discipline to remain invested in the market during periods of market declines.

- Sequence of returns risk and annual withdrawal rates can significantly change outcomes for individual investors.

- Please see the "Probability of Meeting Income Needs" chart on page 57 to see how higher withdrawal rates from an all-equity portfolio can significantly lower the chances of your retirement assets lasting over a 25-year period.

The author and publisher designed this publication to provide expert and useful information regarding the subject covered. However, the author and publisher do not provide legal, financial, or other professional advice with the sale of this publication. Laws and practices vary from country to country. If you need legal or other expert help, you should seek the services of a professional. The author and the publisher disclaim any liability that is incurred from the use or application of the contents of this book.

BLUE MOUNTAIN FINANCIAL GROUP

Blue Mountain Financial Group is affiliated with PFS investments, Inc., A subsidiary of Primerica, Inc., and offer products and services through PFS investments, Inc.

Investors should carefully consider the investment objectives, risks, charges, fees, and expenses of any mutual fund before investing. This and other important information can be found in the funds perspective, and, if available, the summary perspective. Please read the perspective and, if available, the summary perspective carefully before investing. Prospectuses are available from your Primerica representative.

Primerica representatives are not an estate planner, or tax advisor. For related advice, individuals should consult an appropriately, licensed professional.

Cover design by Debraj Dey
Layout by Lilian
Edited by Sean Thomas
Back cover photo by Lauren (Wesleyworks)
Printed in Canada
ISBN 979-8-9919212-0-6

Dedication

To my incredible wife, Bonnie, of 48 years – your unbelievable support from the very start has been a cornerstone of our journey together. We have always been focused on business; in fact, we only took a few days off to get married and skipped a honeymoon to jump straight back into work. You ran our household fully, taking care of the kids and supporting me in every way. Your dedication to our business, especially in those early days with Primerica, was invaluable. I don't always tell you how much I appreciate everything you do but, I truly value you and your efforts so much in creating the success that we have. You helped build the foundation of our success with your natural ability to connect with people, balancing my A-type personality with your relationship-building skills. You've always been my partner in every sense of the word.

To my son, Blake – words can't capture how proud I am of the man you've become. The day you were born was one of the happiest days of my life. Our bond is something truly special, and watching you overcome your challenges has been nothing short of inspiring. Your journey from struggle to success, your discipline in writing your goals every day, and your commitment to staying sober have shown me what true resilience looks like. You've turned your life around in ways that continue to inspire me and so many others. You've found your voice and are now sharing it with the world through your daily podcast – a testament to your strength, determination, and growth.

To my daughter, Brittany – the love I feel for you is endless. As a mother, a talented singer and songwriter, you excel at everything you put your mind to. Your courage to face personal challenges and rise above them is inspiring. Becoming a certified life coach through a renowned global organization speaks volumes about your dedication to helping others become their best. You've shown me time and again what it means to be strong, creative, and compassionate. You're on the road to building something remarkable with your life.

This book is dedicated to you all – Bonnie, Blake, and Brittany – who have shaped me, supported me, and made every step of this journey worthwhile. Your love and strength continue to inspire me every day.

Acknowledgements

I am deeply grateful to the many individuals who have supported and influenced me throughout my journey. Without their guidance, encouragement, and expertise, this book and my career would not have been possible.

A special thank you to the **Boy Scouts of America**, where I earned my Eagle Scout award, one of the merit badges was public speaking where I gained invaluable lessons in public speaking. The discipline and skills I learned as the youngest Eagle Scout in Pennsylvania have been foundational to my personal and professional growth.

A special thank you to my sister and my brother-in law, **Diane** and **Tom Wentz**, for your partnership in two businesses that have been great stepping stones—full of hard work, fun, growth, and valuable lessons.

To **Bob Safford**, who has been like a second father to me. Over the course of 25 years of direct coaching, I have learned more from Bob than I can possibly express. His wisdom and mentorship have shaped much of my approach to business and life.

My heartfelt gratitude to **Art Williams**, whose leadership, mental toughness, and commitment to his crusade changed my life over the three years he coached me. His impact has been immeasurable.

Thank you to **Nick Murray**, author of *Simple Wealth, Inevitable Wealth*. Nick's insights into the 100% equities philosophy and the tools he provided me early on helped me launch and grow my business, especially during a challenging market downturn.

Tom Safford, who continues to honor his father's legacy by coaching and supporting me in my business – thank you for your ongoing friendship and mentorship.

A sincere thank you to **Dean Berger**, who has been instrumental in building our asset allocation mixes for mutual funds, annuities and manged accounts based on my nine baskets strategy.

To **Lavona Berger**, my trusted office manager for 30 years – your loyalty, dedication, and organizational skills have been essential to the success of my business.

I am also incredibly grateful to all my **Regional Vice-Presidents**, whose hard work and commitment have played a crucial role in growing my business. Without them, none of this would be possible.

A huge thank you to **Primerica**, and specifically to **Glenn Williams, Peter Schneider, Bobby Peterman**, and the entire home office team, whose continuous improvements and innovations make our business better every day.

To **Matt and Sally Kacar**, one of our first recruits in Primerica 38 years ago – thank you for your belief in me and for being part of this journey from the very beginning.

Finally, I would like to express my deepest appreciation to **Dr. Denis Cauvier** and his world-class team, whose coaching and guidance were invaluable throughout the writing and publishing process.

This book would not be what it is without the support and mentorship of these incredible individuals. Thank you all for your contributions to my success and for helping me make this dream a reality.

Table of Contents

Foreword

It has been my great fortune to call Ron Weber my friend and business colleague for over 30 years. Not only is he a true superstar in the financial services industry, but even more importantly, he has consistently shown that you don't have to compromise on family values and commitments to achieve business success.

As you turn these pages, you'll get a feel for Ron's warmth and approachable nature, and I know you'll appreciate his self-deprecating humor. He has a knack for putting complex ideas into simple terms, making this journey through financial insights both engaging and enlightening.

Ron has pinpointed financial illiteracy and lack of education as primary contributors to the financial challenges facing North Americans today. He has made it his personal mission to bring about real change in this area. His *Investment Philosophy for Wealth* serves as a masterclass in achieving financial success, providing a clear, step-by-step guide to making progress toward personal wealth. The subtitle of his book, "Mastering Time & Money to Join the Top 2%," promises exactly what he delivers: practical strategies to leverage your time and money and rise to the top 2% of net worth individuals.

Ron's work has transformed the lives of thousands – from novices taking their first steps in financial planning to seasoned experts in the field. Perhaps his most admirable quality is his generosity with his time and expertise; he continually goes above and beyond for his clients, team, family, and friends.

I'm proud to say that my son and business partner, Brett, and I are among the many people who have been deeply influenced by Ron's friendship and coaching.

So, dive in and enjoy this journey with Ron as he shares his *Investment Philosophy for Wealth*. His insights could be the very key you need to unlock your financial potential.

Mike Wooten - Senior National Sales Director, Primerica

Message from the author

Dear Reader,

American household debt reached a record $17.8 trillion in Q2 2024, with nearly 600 million credit card accounts, while inflation continues to strain budgets. Financial literacy is also on the decline – only 34% of 27,000 adults in a recent FINRA (the Financial Industry Regulatory Authority) survey could answer basic financial questions, down from 40% in 2000. As a result, many Americans are financially illiterate, and Millennials are facing the worst retirement prospects of any generation.

When I founded Blue Mountain Financial Group, my aim was crystal clear: to help families become more financially literate and to break free from the conventional norms of the financial industry and pave a path that puts clients first. Over the years, I've crafted a distinct investment philosophy and system designed to empower individuals like you to build and preserve wealth for retirement, regardless of your starting point.

In the traditional landscape, retirement strategies often lean on a mix of stocks and bonds, gradually shifting towards more conservative allocations as retirement approaches. At Blue Mountain Financial Group however, we take a bold stance by focusing exclusively on equity-based investments. Our approach revolves around strategic asset class diversification, harnessing dividend income, and employing protective measures such as variable annuities to temper risk and volatility.

This philosophy isn't just theoretical – it's rooted in over 38 years of hands-on experience. I've dedicated myself to understanding market dynamics and tailoring personalized investment plans that align with your unique circumstances and aspirations. Beyond crafting strategies, I place significant emphasis on coaching you through the journey, emphasizing the value of staying invested rather than attempting to time the market.

As of the publication of this book, Blue Mountain Financial Group and my Primerica team proudly supports over half a billion dollars of client assets under management. This milestone isn't just a number; it symbolizes the trust and confidence our clients have placed in us to steward their financial futures.

Whether you're just starting to build your nest egg or fine-tuning your retirement plans, I'm committed to helping you achieve your financial goals with clarity and conviction. At Blue Mountain Financial Group, our dedication remains unwavering – we're here to champion your financial well-being every step of the way.

Warm regards,
Ronald Weber, Founder, Blue Mountain Financial Group - National Sales Director, Primerica

Introduction

How many of you want to be wealthy if you could? Is that important to you? The shocking truth is that, right now, only 2% actually achieve wealth. Charles Schwab defines wealthy as having $2.5 million dollars of net worth. So, it's not normal for most people to achieve wealth in retirement. But, in this book, I want to show you exactly what I've learned about how to create wealth, and what I've been able to teach to other people. There are only two resources available to create wealth, one is how you invest your time and the second is how you invest your money: Investing your time involves what you do with your time to make money, such as trading your time for money with a job or as someone who is self-employed. It's critical to understand because how you invest your time dictates if you even have enough money to invest. Eighty-five percent of Americans are employees, and as such they are paid based on their position, not their worth as individuals. Most employees never make enough money to cover all their expenses and have enough left over to invest. Self-employed people own their job, which amounts to trading their hours for dollars. The problem is that the more money you want to make, the more hours you have to work. That is not freedom.

The best way to invest your time is to be a business owner. This is where you own a system and have people working for you, all of which you make income off of, even when you are not working, i.e., when you're sick, sleeping, or on holiday, etc. Finally, an investor is someone whose money is making money without them putting in any additional effort. The fast-track to becoming wealthy is to own a successful business and start investing money right away. You might be surprised to know that 60% of Americans right now are actively looking to go into business for themselves. The Covid pandemic gave people a little taste of freedom. Some people got paid more money not to work than to work because of the stimulus checks that they received. And a lot of people thought that was pretty cool. They didn't have to go to work and they still got paid a lot of money, and they liked that. So now, some people are realizing they don't want to go back to work. They would like to maybe start their own business, and that includes some of you reading this book. So, I want to make sure that I convey to you the importance of being in business for yourself.

Some of you are already investors trying to build wealth. And now, with all the hoopla that you've heard recently, you're probably wondering what is going on with our country. You're thinking, "Are we going to be okay?" Some of you are just looking at the idea of wealth-building for the very first time. You have money, but you're not getting the returns you should really make on your money, and you would like to learn more about how to get better rates of return. So, my goal with this book is to address the concerns of each and every one of you. And I want to begin by introducing myself and my story.

My Story

I am the founder and owner of a company called Blue Mountain Financial Group and a National Sales Director of Primerica, the largest financial services marketing organization in North America. Before I discuss further what I currently do as a financial advisor, I want to go back to my early days, as these previous experiences have all led me to where I am today.

First of all, I graduated with a health and phys. ed. degree. Guys like me should not be wealthy, right? But the truth is, it has nothing to do with what your education or profession is. It has to do with the knowledge you acquire and the people that mentor you along the way. And, I've been grateful that I had some very key influential people that literally changed my life. But my initial goal was to be a professional football player. I was good, but not good enough, just like a lot of other people. But I loved sports. That was my whole life. And along the way, I got married during college. So then I had a wife who wanted to eat every now and then, so I couldn't indulge my love of sports for nothing. But I loved the aspect of coaching people.

The year was 1977 I was offered a teaching job right where I student taught paying $12,000 a year. I clearly recall a life-changing conversation with Mr. Hershey, the school principal, about my job as a teacher. At the end of our conversation, he asked me, "Ron, do you have any specific questions or aspirations? What is it you're really looking to do?" My goal was to be wealthy, but I didn't think I was smart enough. I asked him if he could name four teachers that would retire wealthy from that school so I could talk to them and then do what they did. To my surprise, he said **none** of them would retire wealthy. So then I asked him, "What about you, being the principal and one of the highest paid people?" He told me that he, too, would not retire wealthy. I thought to myself, "If the people at the top aren't getting wealthy, what's the point of staying here?" That's when it hit me – I had to rethink my approach.

My ultimate goal was always to be wealthy. So I started looking up information: Who are these people who are wealthy? What do they look like? What do they do? Back then – this was 1977 when I graduated – I found that 94% of Americans worked for the other 6% who owned businesses. Out of the 5% that created financial independence or wealth, 90% of them came from the 6% that owned businesses. Only 10% came from the workforce. So I said, well, if I want a nine times better chance of creating wealth and independence, then I've got to put myself in a business situation.

I always thought you either work for someone who owns a business, or you own the business yourself. I didn't realize there was actually a middle step, which is something you have to go through before you get to be a business owner, called self-employed.

Because I didn't know that, I spent ten years of my life wandering around, not really knowing where I was going. I was making a 6 figure income but spending most of it on business expenses. I was just broke at a higher level because of the typical pitfalls – like the guy who used to call the wrong number, not realizing it was the wrong number.

One of the most impactful books I have read is, **Rich Dad's Cashflow Quadrant** by Robert Kiyosaki. To reach the top 2% financially, it's all about mastering both your time and money. The **Four Cashflow Quadrants** show how people earn income, but the goal is to shift from working for money to making money work for you.

In the **Employee (E)** quadrant, you trade your time for a paycheck. It's unstable, because someone else controls your time and money. Ultimately you are working in a pyramid system where to get ahead the person above you has to quit, die or get fired to move up. To move beyond this you should, focus on maximizing your job's earning potential and start building wealth through smart investments.

In the **Self-Employed (S)** quadrant, you're your own boss, but you're still tied to your time. It's critical to note that the more successful you become the harder you have to work! To break free, you need to systematize your business so it doesn't require your constant effort – hire, delegate, and scale.

In the **Business Owner (B)** quadrant, you've built a system or team that makes money for you. Your focus is on growth, strategy, and leveraging other people's time to create more income. This is where you start to master both time and money.

Finally, in the **Investor (I)** quadrant, your money works for you. You invest in assets like real estate or stocks that generate passive income, building wealth over time with minimal effort.

To become part of the top 2%, move from the E and S quadrants to the B and I quadrants. Focus on creating scalable income streams and building assets that generate passive income. That's the key to financial freedom – letting your money and time work for you.

When you look at business, it's actually very simple. All business deals with a product, service or idea. To be successful, it's about finding a need and filling it. The greater the need, the more money you can make by fulfilling it. I have found there are 3 ways to get into business (starting a business from scratch with a C-Corp, franchising or building a company within a company) Let me show you a couple of examples.

Example 1: one of my first ventures I started with my brother-in-law called Weber-Wentz Auto Brokerage Firm. I thought, "Everyone drives a car, right?" Back in the late '70s, car leasing was becoming popular. Cars were expensive, and leasing made monthly payments more manageable, but you didn't actually own the car unless you bought it out at the end of the lease.

I bought into a company called "Engage A Car." It wasn't your typical car dealership – this one had an engagement ring logo with a car going through the middle of it. It was a fun, creative concept (why marry your car, engage it). After leasing a new Chevy Blazer to my dad, I ordered a second car for my sister's boyfriend, that car never arrived. After making numerous calls to find out what was going on I drove to Cherry Hill, New Jersey to the main office where I did my training – but when I got there, I found out that the company had gone out of business.

So, I always tell people: **Never do business with a company whose main office is a hotel room.** Thus, pitfall number 1: **getting involved with the wrong company**.

From this experience, I learned a key lesson: if you want to truly be a business owner and create residual income – money that keeps coming in long after you've put in the work – you have to make sure the company or model you're involved with has that long-term sustainability.

Example 2: we started another company in the early '80s called **Vidtronics Inc.** This was a coin operated amusement business. At the time, I was a total video game nut. I loved arcade games – Ms. Pac-Man, Donkey Kong, you name it. I figured, if I'm spending all this money playing these machines, I might as well own them. So I did. We ended up owning a thousand arcade machines, with a whopping $57,000 a month mortgage payment to cover.

For a while, it was great. We even opened one of the biggest arcades on the East Coast, called the Supercade, right on the boardwalk in Wildwood, New Jersey. It was a huge success. At one point, the arcade was making enough to cover our mortgage payments on its own. But, here's the catch – it was a fad. The arcade game boom, with hits like **Ms. Pac-Man** and **Donkey Kong**, burned bright, but it didn't last. Technology moved fast, and we were always scrambling to keep up. What seemed like a hot business turned out to be unsustainable in the long run.

That's when I realized: while it's fun to ride trends, if you want long-term success, you have to pick a business model that can stand the test of time – not one that's just a flash in the pan. Thus, pitfall number 2: **getting involved with the wrong product**.

Example 3: I started a franchise called Life Safety Systems, which sold a new product called the Sargom Fire Extinguisher. It was revolutionary. It would put out fires and leave no mess. But it didn't have UL approval. I sold millions of dollars by franchising it, but then it got to the point where some of my distributors were telling me I needed to get some type of endorsement because it was tough to market this type of product without the UL approval. Today Sargom gas is used in most computer rooms in the country because of its ability to put out fires and have no residue mess. The real issue was that I was ahead of my time; the computer industry really didn't take off until the 90s, but I had started the company in the 80s. Thus, pitfall number 3: **getting involved at the wrong time**.

Example 4: the other side of franchising, where we were a franchisee was KOA campgrounds. My family brought the first one to the East Coast back in 1968. A good business should net you about 15% in profits per month. But we were paying 11% to KOA, leaving us with only 4%! So, basically we were just scraping by working for ourselves. The problem was compounded by the fact that being in the northeast of America meant that 90% of our season was between Memorial Day and Labor Day, even though our costs were year round. Pitfall number 4: **getting involved with the wrong location**!

FIG. 1: KOA CAMPGROUND

Then my wife and I bought the second location, which the franchise illegally built in our territory, so we ended up putting it out of business and purchased it from a local farmer. That was the longest business we had – 8 years, probably because my wife ran it. We took a bankrupt business that was doing 400 camper nights to 4,000, and we were rocking. We worked our asses off. We were working seven days a week to try to make things happen in our business.

After eight years, I decided to take a hunting trip – something I'd always wanted to do – an elk hunt down in Colorado. I had never left the business for all those years. I had a great time hunting and on the last night, back at the base camp, I talked to my wife and said, "I'll be home tomorrow." And then around two o'clock in the morning, I got a phone call. They told me, "Your wife's on the phone. It's an emergency." That's when my wife told me there had been a fire. She told me the main building was okay, but we had lost the apartment. I said it wasn't a big deal. We'd put a trailer on the side. We'd be rocking and rolling again in no time. We'd be fine. The next day my wife picked me up at the airport. She said, "You'll never guess what happened." I said, "What the heck could be worse than that?" She said, "It rekindled at six o'clock in the morning." They called the fire department, which was a volunteer fire department. It took them two hours to respond, and it burned to the ground.

FIG. 2: AFTER THE FIRE

We lost everything we owned. You want to talk about being devastated? We were not properly insured, because you never think things like this will ever happen to you. So we were very frustrated. It was very tempting to just have a little pity party about what happened to us. It's very easy to do that. But, here's one of the things I've learned in business: with every adversity, there's a seed of greater benefit if you're looking for it. So, a couple of weeks after this fire, a man named Jack Brixius called me. Jack is a friend of ours who had moved to Florida. He was part of American Can, which is part of Primerica's early history. Jack said, "Hey, Alice and I will be up in the area. We'd like to get together with you and Bonnie."

I told him we don't have the Kutztown KOA anymore. We ended up selling it for land value because we couldn't afford to rebuild the building. Then he asked me, "What are you going to do with the money, Ron?"

I said, "You know, Jack, I'm probably going to buy a McDonald's franchise now."

I really valued his opinion because I knew he was financially free. So here's what he said to me: "What the hell are you going to do that for?" I said, Jack, I'm a hardworking guy. I know I can make a 12% return on my time because I'm a hard worker. He said, how would you like to make that kind of money without lifting a finger?

I said, "Come on. If it's that easy, everybody would do it."

And he said, "I retired wealthy. You ever wonder how I did it?"

Yes, I did. Maybe you've heard the saying, *when the student's ready, the teacher appears.* Well, that's what happened. He started talking to me about mutual funds. I knew nothing about investing money. Zero. But I listened to what he told me to do, and I made more money in eight months in that investment than I did running my business all year long. I was absolutely blown away by that. And, then he introduced us to A.L. Williams, which became Primerica. He said there's a guy that accounts for 10% of the company's business, named Bob Safford, and you should go down and talk to him. And we thank God every single day for what he did for us. The reason why Primerica worked, is we could use their billions in assets without having to pay a franchise fee. We could build a company within a company. When we got big they got bigger.

And that was my ticket. I started at 31, became a millionaire before I was 40 years old, and now we are multimillionaires many times over. We became the company's 136th million-dollar-a-year income earners. Today we live on a 22-acre horse ranch with our kids – our son Blake, daughter Brittany, – and our grandkids all live on our property. When you create wealth, your kids never leave. In fact not only do they come back, they bring a bunch of others with them!

FIG. 3: KATIE, OLIVE, TANYA, FALLON, BLAKE, SOLYN, RON 'PAPPY", LUKE, BONNIE 'BABA' AND BRITTANY

FIG. 4: OUR 22-ACRE HORSE RANCH

I don't say that to brag by any stretch of the imagination. I say that because if someone like us can do it, *you* can do it. That's my whole point.

We explored many entrepreneurial ventures in our pursuit of financial success, but often found ourselves either with the wrong product or using the wrong distribution model. However, when we discovered Primerica, we found the right combination of products, support system, and distribution model. What's fascinating about Primerica is that while you're in business for yourself, you're never by yourself.

As I mentioned earlier, there are two primary ways to make money: either by working for it or by having your money work for you. Smart investing is all about the latter. Primerica blends these two principles by teaching you how to make your money work for you, while also offering a proven business system where you can generate income by educating others on financial fundamentals.

One of the things that we really liked about Primerica is that it incorporates the best aspects of starting a business from scratch, buying an existing business, franchising, direct marketing, and even large corporations – without the typical downsides of these models. Primerica is based on offering personalized advice on how to invest money wisely. And, for those who don't have enough capital to invest, they offer a part-time or full-time business opportunity to make money while helping other families get their finances in order.

I started Blue Mountain Financial Group because I wanted to be independent of the industry. I had gotten very frustrated that the things I was learning financially don't work anymore. So, in this book, you're going to hear some things that I'm not even "supposed to" tell you, according to FINRA and some of the other big industry players. But, I'm to the point where I want people to know the truth. I want people to know why things aren't working. Because, if you are investing for your retirement now – and that's what a lot of people are looking for – if you're 55 to 65 years old, that means you're only a few steps away from retirement.

According to the article "What do working Americans fear more than death? Retirement." Many Americans are not only financially not prepared to retire – some fear retirement more than death, a recent survey shows. About 61% of working Americans are more afraid of retiring then dying, and 64% fear retirement more than getting divorced according to national survey for LiveCareer in June 2024.

Are You Retirement Ready?

How much do you have in your retirement account? And, how much do you need? In fact, Fidelity and Vanguard have just put out two great reports. Vanguard's was the "How America Saves" report, and Fidelity's report was "How Much Do I Need to Retire?" Isn't that a fear for most people who are turning age 65? Do I have enough money to retire? Am I going to be able to make it? How much is enough? Well, the report from Fidelity says if you retire at age 67 – which is pretty much what we consider the full Social Security age today – then what you need to retire on is 10 times your annual salary. So let's say you have a spouse and both of you are working – you're probably making around a $100,000 a year between the two of you.

And so, Fidelity says at retirement you need $1 million, or 10 times your annual earnings. Vanguard asked, how are we doing in terms of reaching this goal? The average retirement account for someone 55 to 64 years old today has a balance of $84,714. You see there is a huge disconnect. The issue is that people do not have anywhere near enough money to be able to live a comfortable retirement. And, that's very frightening for a lot of people. One of the reasons for this situation is that the things people have been told about investing for retirement don't work anymore for one simple reason – we live too long. There was a great article published by AARP called "Live to 100. Plan on It," and I will quote from it here:

> Jeanne Calment was a typical woman of her time. Born in Arles, France in 1875, she lived a rather unremarkable life by most accounts except for one thing – when she died in 1997 at the age of 122, she was on record as the oldest person ever to have lived. "I just kept getting older and couldn't help it," she once said. So what does the extraordinary life of this ordinary woman have to do with us today? More than you might think. In her day, living to a hundred was extremely rare. But today in the United States people 100 and over represent the second fastest-growing age group in our country. The fastest? People over 85. Many 65-year-olds today will live well into their nineties. Think of it another way: a 10-year-old child today – maybe your grandchild – has a 50% chance of living to 104. Some demographers have even speculated that the first person ever to live to 150 is alive today.

People who will live to 150 may be already here walking on the planet! Is that scary? One thing I want you to realize right out front is you're going to spend more money in retirement than you earn during your whole working life. And, that should be very frightening for a bunch of people.

A Simple, Life-Changing Rule

Now that you've heard a bit of my story, you are probably wondering what is the one key I learned earlier on to create wealth. The very first rule I learned, in fact I practically built a whole business on just explaining this one rule that made so many of my clients and me wealthy – is called the "Rule of 72." And, how does the rule of 72 work? It's really simple: whatever rate of return your money earns, if you divide 72 by that number, that tells you approximately how long it will take for your money to double. Let's say you make 3%, a typical rate of return from a bank – 72 divided by 3 is 24. That means you will double your money in 24 years. So, if you have $10,000 and you put it in the bank, 24 years later it's grown to $20,000. And, in 48 years, it's grown to $40,000. Now, what happens to your money after 48 years if you double the interest rate? You might expect that you would double your money. Except money doesn't work like that. As you can see in Figure 5, at 6% return the money's doubling every 12 years. So in 48 years, it's not $80,000 but $160,000. And just look what happens at 12%.

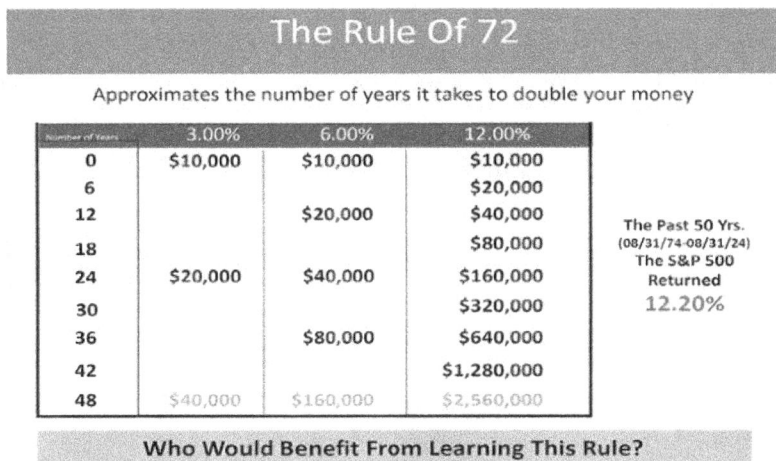

The Rule Of 72

Approximates the number of years it takes to double your money

Number of Years	3.00%	6.00%	12.00%	
0	$10,000	$10,000	$10,000	
6			$20,000	
12		$20,000	$40,000	The Past 50 Yrs.
18			$80,000	(08/31/74-08/31/24)
24	$20,000	$40,000	$160,000	The S&P 500
30			$320,000	Returned
36		$80,000	$640,000	12.20%
42			$1,280,000	
48	$40,000	$160,000	$2,560,000	

Who Would Benefit From Learning This Rule?

FIG. 5: THE RULE OF 72

At a 12% return, the money's doubling every six years. So you can see that in 48 years that $10,000 will be $2,560,000. The fact is, depositing your money in the bank will never get you 12%. So, for those of you that continue keeping your money in the bank, I just have one question: Why are you doing this? If you leave a $10,000 nest egg in the bank for 48 years, you just gave away $2,560,000. Another way to look at this is for every $10,000 you deposit in a bank over a 48-year period you are losing out on another

$2,560,000. So ask yourself: how many times can you give away $2,560,000 and not be broke in retirement?

You may be wondering where do you make the kind of returns I'm talking about? Is it even possible to get a 12% return? Well, let me give you an example. Over the past 50 years, the average return in the market, based on the S&P 500, is 12.2%. So again, if you had $10,000 invested in the market for the past 48 years, you're right there over $2,500,000 today. These are life-changing numbers. And, what I do, is show people how simple our business really is. We say, "Here's the rate of return you're getting. How would you like to move your money over and possibly get a 12% return? Anybody interested in something like that?" That's a no-brainer. People are not stupid. People are just financially ignorant. If you educate them, they're going to do the right thing.

When you look at it, you see that the rate of return is obviously the key. So, I want to go back even further with data. And when you look to invest, there are basically three asset classes you can invest in. You could invest in cash, which would be something like a certificate of deposit (CD). And, what I tell people about CDs is that there has seldom been a time in history when a CD made money after you factor in taxes and inflation. So, I'm blown away by fact that there's $18 trillion of people's money sitting in bank accounts today making little to no money. That makes no sense to me. And, when I find people who are doing that, the first thing I ask them is, "Why?" And, they usually give me two reasons. Number one is that it's guaranteed. Do you know what I say to that? I say, yes, it's guaranteed – to lose you money!

Compounded Annualized Total Returns, 1926-2023

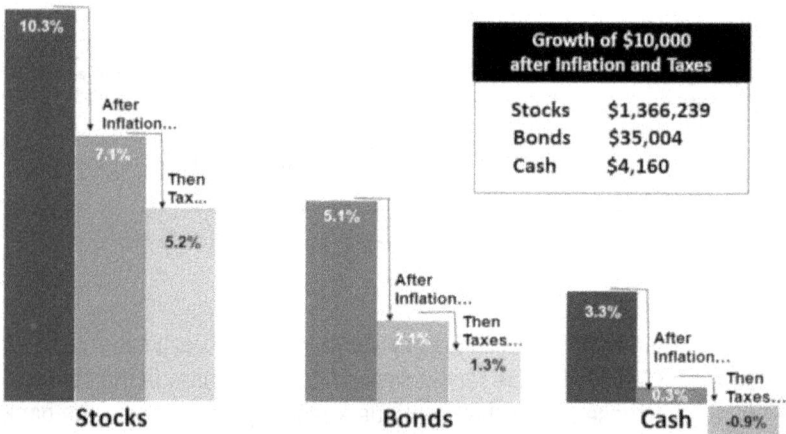

Growth of $10,000 after Inflation and Taxes	
Stocks	$1,366,239
Bonds	$35,004
Cash	$4,160

FIG. 6: RATE OF RETURN IS KEY

Let's look at what happens when you factor in taxes and inflation. In Figure 6, I'm going all the way back to 1926, so we're looking at a period of 97 years. If you put $10,000 into a CD in 1926, 97 years later, after taxes and inflation, your $10,000 is worth $4,160. Do you think that's a smart move financially? (Remember this saying: "Either your *assets* are at work, or your *ass* is at work.")

And, the other thing people tell me is, "Well, I know where my money is." And I say, "Have you ever noticed when you walk in the bank that the vault is open? Why is that? It's because your money is not there. I can tell you where it is, though. The banks are reinvesting it for a much higher rate of return, mostly right in the market. You could have done that yourself (for as little as $25), but you didn't because no one ever taught you how to do that. Because they want you to be very fearful of the market." They say, "Oh, you don't want to be in the market because you could lose your money." And yet your money is in their CD where you have been guaranteed to lose?

The second asset class where you can put your money is bonds. When you look at bonds in Figure 6, you can see that after taxes and inflation your $10,000 investment in bonds is worth $34,004 after 97 years. And, the third type of investment you can make is stocks, or equities. After taxes and inflation, 97 years later your $10,000 is worth $1,366,239.

You've heard the expression, "Don't put all your eggs in one basket." You will often hear this advice applied to your investment strategy. The industry says you should have so much in stock, so much in bonds, and so much in cash. You want to have something like a 50/40/10 portfolio. Now, remember, I graduated with a phys. ed. degree and got hit in the head a lot of times, so, maybe I'm not thinking straight. But, here's what I think: why would I want to put any money in an account that I know is going to lose me money? Does that make any sense to you whatsoever?

And, here's the thing about stocks and bonds. Typically when stocks go up, bonds go down. When stocks go down, bonds go up. So if I have a 50/40 mix, that means the 40% of my money in bonds is canceling out 40% of my equity investment. I would only have 10% of my money that's making money. Is it any wonder there is only $84,714 in the retirement account of the average 55-64 year old? This investment strategy never made any sense to me. So, what I did was put all my money into the equity market. Now, in fact there are nine different baskets of equities you want to put your money into, so you're not really putting all your eggs in one basket. I will talk about those nine equity baskets later. But if you want to achieve wealth right now, you don't want to divide your investments between these three baskets of stocks, bonds, and cash.

Nominal and real U.S. 10-year Treasury yields

	Average (1958 - present)	Aug. 14, 2024
Nominal yields	5.74%	3.83%
Real yields	1.93%	0.62%
Inflation	3.81%	3.21%

Sep. 30, 1981: 15.84%

Nominal 10-year U.S. Treasury yield

Real 10-year U.S. Treasury yield

Aug. 14, 2024: 3.83%

Aug. 14, 2024: 0.62%

Source: BLS, FactSet, Federal Reserve, J.P. Morgan Asset Management.
Real 10-year Treasury yields are calculated as the daily Treasury yield less year-over-year core CPI inflation for that month. For the current month, we use the prior month's core CPI figures until the latest data are available.
Guide to the Markets – U.S. Data are as of August 14, 2024.

J.P.Morgan
ASSET MANAGEMENT

FIG. 7: INTEREST RATES AND INFLATION

In Figure 7, we can see the nominal and real yields of bonds. Let's talk about the real yield, after inflation, of bonds right now in August 2024. You can see the bond yield right now is 0.6%. Let's plug that into the rule of 72 and see how many years it would take to double our money. Remember, according to the rule of 72, if we have a 1% return, it would take 72 years (72 divided by 1 equals 72). If we're getting 0.6%, that means it would take 120 years for our money to double. Do you have that long? It's pretty crazy to think you can get to where you need to be using bonds.

The Stock Market

The US stock market has been around since 1792, 16 years after our country was founded. It started with 24 stockbrokers sitting around a buttonwood tree at 68 Wall Street, New York, at the southern end of Manhattan. It was getting so big so fast that they could no longer conduct their business casually under a tree – they needed a proper space and some formal rules, so they signed the Buttonwood Agreement. And, years later, that became the New York Stock Exchange, now the biggest exchange in the world. Today the global market capitalization is $109 trillion, and the United States accounts for 42.5% of that, or about $46 trillion. That's huge!

In Figure 8 you can see the market returns over the last 10 years. In the bottom row of the table, on the right, you can see that so far this year the market return is 19.53%. Just above that you can see we hit 26.29% in 2023. We were down 18.11% in 2022 because we went into a bear market that year. That's the way the market works: seven steps forward, one step back. Seven forward, one back. That's normal. But look at the returns from the three years before that. (28.71%, 18.40%, 39.49%)

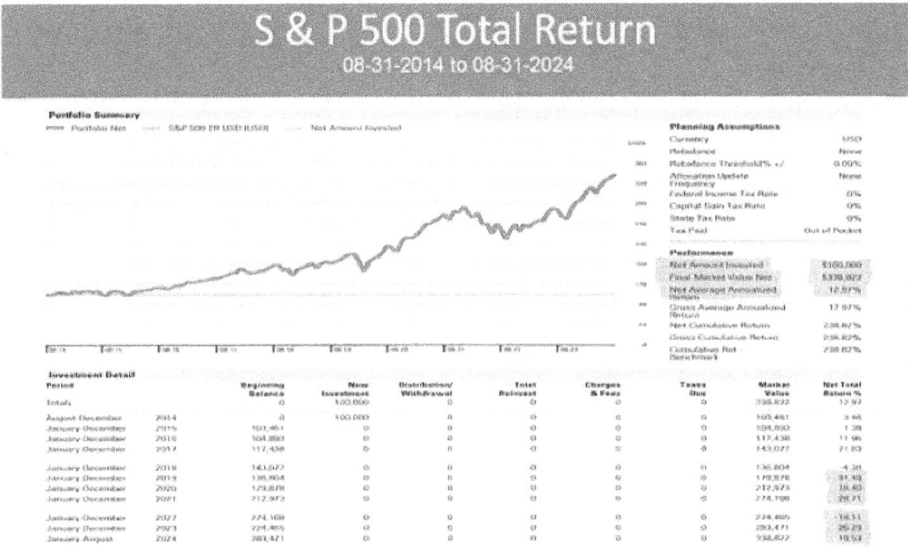

FIG. 8: S&P 500 RETURNS, 2014-2024

What would have happened if you put $100,000 into the market 10 years ago? A lot of things have happened during that time. Remember, in 2018 President Trump said they were not going to raise the debt ceiling, they would let the government shut down, the whole nine yards. And, of course, that affected some of the returns in that year. Then we had Covid in there, and then that bear market in 2022. With all of that, if you put a $100,000 in there 10 years ago, you would now have $338,822 based on an average return of 12.97% a year. Is that pretty cool?

Right now, people have so much fear about going into the market. On August the 5th the S&P 500 experienced a one-day drop of 3%, and lots of people were panicking about that. One of the things that you have to understand is that a lot of the response to things that are going on is emotional. I wish school had prepared us all better to understand money and markets, which would be so much more useful than a lot of things we learned. We all had algebra in school, but how many of us use algebra to make a living? Nobody, unless you are a math teacher. On the other hand, very few of us learned about money in school, yet we deal with money matters every single day of our lives. That means that when it comes to money, people operate on emotion, not logic, because they don't have any education about money. And, when it comes to the markets, anytime you operate on emotion you're going to get your butt kicked.

Let me prove it. On August 5th of this year, we had what many described as a market panic. I'm going to quote from an article about it published by Stansberry Research:

> Fear is back...
>
> When the US market opened this morning, panic could be seen all over. The CBOE volatility index ("VIX") – what some considered the market's fear gauge, a measure of option activity on the S&P 500 Index – spiked from below 20 for most of last week to above 60 this morning. That's its highest level outside of the Covid-19 panic in March of 2020 and the onset of the great financial crisis in 2008.

Just to give you some extra insight on that, a couple of days later it was revealed that the VIX didn't really hit 65. The apparent spike to that was due entirely to the mis-pricing of a single option which threw the VIX calculation widely out of wack. The VIX actually hit 32, not 65 according to the data complied by Bloomberg. Is that crazy? People reacted to information that wasn't even true. But let me continue with the article:

> The major US indexes were down by 3% or more across the board... Treasury yields were down (meaning bond prices were up)... Bitcoin briefly traded below $50,000... Even gold was down 2%...
>
> The NASDAQ Composite Index and S&P 500 were down 2.9%. The small-cap Russell 2000 Index was off 3.2%, and the Dow Jones Industrial Average was off 2.6%. This

was the first "everything is down" day like this since the early days of the bear market of 2022 or the pandemic panic if you want to use volatility as a marker. ...

It didn't even take that much to trigger a sell-off...

That's right, it didn't take much. Just some negative US manufacturing and jobs data for July. But, as the article goes on to say, "It was like a pin in the bubble. Add it all up and last week's jobs reports were significant enough to get enough investors thinking seriously about the prospect of a US recession ahead."

So fear was driving investors. But guess what? Ten days later, everything was back to normal. I mean everything was back to where it was before all that panic happened. So here's the question: Is it possible that we investors, because we operate on emotion and not logic, could drive ourselves into a recession? Yes, it's possible. Because we're financially uneducated. We follow the media and we get a bunch of hype. That's what moves things right now.

But, let's look at what's really happening now. If you look at Figure 9, you can see that in years when we've had a strong first quarter, anything over 10% return, the next three quarters have had a positive return 10 times out of 11. And look at this year, 2024 – the rate of return in the first quarter was 10.2%.

Strong First Quarter Returns: A Historical Prelude to Continued Strength

S&P 500 returns in years where Q1 gained at least 10% (1950- 2024)

Year	First Quarter Return	Return in Next 3 Quarters	Full Year Return
1961	12.0%	10.0%	23.1%
1967	12.3%	7.0%	20.1%
1975	21.6%	8.2%	31.5%
1976	13.9%	4.6%	19.1%
1986	13.1%	1.4%	14.8%
1987	20.5%	-15.3%	2.0%
1991	13.6%	11.2%	26.3%
1998	13.5%	11.6%	26.7%
2012	12.0%	1.3%	13.4%
2013	10.0%	17.8%	29.6%
2019	13.1%	14.0%	28.9%
2024	10.2%	?	?
Average	14.1%	6.5%	21.4%

What is this chart showing?

This chart shows the years in which the S&P 500 gained at least 10% in the first quarter, as well as the S&P 500 performance for the remainder of the year and full year return.

Why is it important?

Strength often begets strength. The S&P 500 gained 10.2% in the first quarter of 2024. Since 1950, this is the 12th time the index has gained 10% or more in the first three months.

In the previous 11 instances, the index was higher over the remaining three quarters all but one time, with an average additional gain of 6.5%

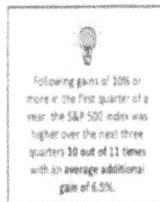

Following gains of 10% or more in the first quarter of a year, the S&P 500 index was higher over the next three quarters 10 out of 11 times with an average additional gain of 6.5%.

Source: Morningstar, Lincoln Financial Group 1950-2023. S&P 500 Price Return index does not include dividends. 2024 not included in average returns. Past performance does not guarantee future results.

Lincoln Investment Advisors

...erica, Inc. and its affiliates are not affiliated with Lincoln Financial or its affiliates ...d with permission

FIG. 9: STRONG 1ST QUARTER RETURNS PREDICT STRONG ANNUAL RETURNS

So, this year we are on track for a good year. Look at the full year returns for all of these years. The average rate of return is 21.4%. We're actually at 19% so far this year, so we are on the right track. But some people look at this and say, "Yeah, but we're at an all-time high." They think that makes it different now. The fact is, putting money to work when the market is at an all-time high has historically performed better than putting your money in when it's below the peak. In other words, when the market is high, the returns are actually higher.

Here's what I want you to realize. Everything we're talking about is fear driven. But what I want you to understand is that we should not be fearful about the market. Today, the Dow Jones Industrial Average is at around 40,000. What if I told you that by 2031, seven years from now, the Dow should hit 150,000? And, do you know why? It's because we are in the greatest decade in history right now. The greatest decade we ever had prior to this was the nineties. At that time, it was fueled by cell phones, personal computers, and the internet. The market quadrupled itself in that decade and the NASDAQ was up 900%. We're now in what they call the roaring 2020s, fueled by two things: One is AI. There are AI companies out there that will be the next tenfold companies that you've never even heard of. And number two is DNA mapping. They believe that by 2030 we'll have a cure for every disease that's out there. Hard to believe, right? I just got back from a Franklin Templeton meeting down in Florida at their main headquarters. I talked to one of our portfolio managers, Mike Clarfeld, who manages Franklin Templeton Dividend Strategy. I asked Mike, "How in the world can you say that they're going to have a cure for every disease?" And he gave me an example about the hereditary disease called spina bifida. He told me there is a company out there now that can take eight eggs from a woman and they can test them to see which of those eggs will carry that disease and which will not. Then they fertilize the one that won't, and put it back in the woman. That is one of the companies you've never heard of at this point that will probably become one of the next tenfold stocks.

What's happening here is absolutely mind blowing. But you have to understand that when you look at the market, everything operates in cycles. And we have two broad types of cycles: cyclical and secular. Cyclical cycles are shorter-term market trends – the typical cycles of growth and contraction that play out over a 12-18 month period. A secular cycle is one that unfolds over a longer time period of 12-18 years, and is not much affected by short-term cyclical trends. If you look at the market going back to 1929, we are actually right now in the third long-term secular bull market (see second, fourth, and last rows in Figure 10"). The first one was from 1949 to 1968, which was 19 years, and the average return in the market was 16%. The second one was 1982 to 2000. That one was 18 years with an average return of 20%. The one we're in now started in 2013. We've been in this secular bull run now for a little over 10 years, and the average return so far is 12.5%.

Timeframe	Length (Years)	Annual Return
1929-1949	20	0%
1949-1968	19	16%
1968-1982	14	4%
1982-2000	18	20%
2000-2013	13	2.5%
2013-Now	10	12.5%

www.stansberryresearch.com

FIG. 10: SECULAR BULL MARKETS SINCE 1929

Based on the previous two, we can assume that the overall return for this one should be 16-20%. By the way, if it hits 16% return, every $10,000 that you have invested over the period of this bull run will be worth $170,000. If the average return for the whole period is 20%, then every $10,000 is worth a $250,000 by 2031. So, if perhaps you haven't saved as much as you should have up to now, you have a window that you could use to make this up in a huge way. Since we are currently at a 12.5% average return for the period since 2013, in order for us to hit 16% average return by 2031, we have to average 21% a year for the next eight years. So, how did we do in 2023, as an example? We did 26%. Seven months into this year, we're at 19% – on track to surpass 21% for the full year. The market is exactly where it needs to be.

If you look back to 2009, when we had the Great Recession, the Dow hit one of its all-time lowest numbers. It dropped all the way to 6,600. March 9th was the low point. That year I had an operation to extend my jaw forward, and I had to wear braces for a year. And my orthodontist, a guy named Dr. Tighe, knew what I did for a living, so he said to me, "Ron, you will never see the Dow hit 10,000 again in our lifetime." It was at 6,600 at that time, but just two years before it had hit an all-time high of 14,000. And yet, my dentist tells me that we'll never see the Dow hit 10,000 in our lifetime. I said, "Thank God you're an orthodontist and not a financial advisor, because you would suck!" What actually happened was the Dow hit 10,000 that same year (October 14, 2009), only seven months after the low of 6,600. On my next visit to the dentist, I brought an article out that said the Dow would hit 30,000 by 2020. That's a five-fold increase from March 2009. And my dentist said to me, "I will bet you my practice that will never happen." Well, when did it go over 30,000? November 24th, 2020. So, people hear this kind of prediction and they say that's impossible. But it's not impossible. It already happened. That should give you hope.

S&P 500 Price Index Since 1956 Bear Market with Recessions Shaded

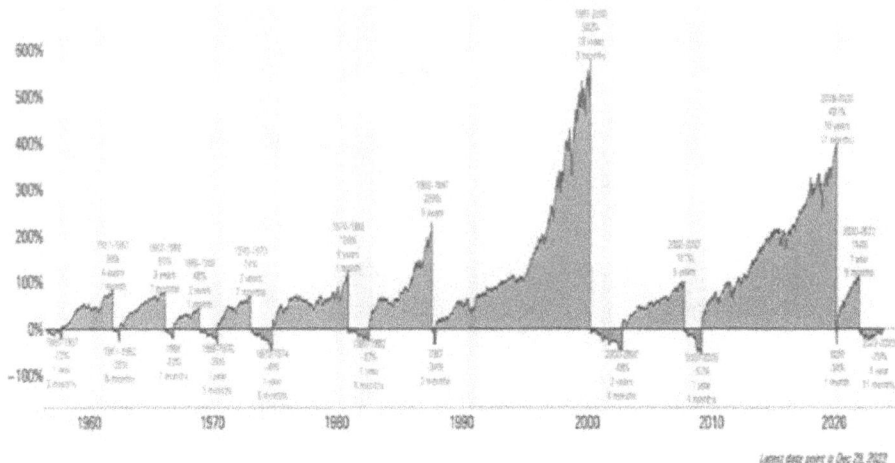

FIG. 11: UNDERSTANDING LONG-TERM INVESTING

I mentioned at the beginning of the book that our company name is Blue Mountain Financial Group. Where did that name come from? If you look at Figure 11 you will see the "rising mountains" right there. On full color graphs of the stock market, the gains are often depicted in the color blue, thus I call them blue mountains of equity growth. (And I also live right next to the Blue Mountain, so there's a neat double meaning there.) But you can see the huge returns that the mountains on this graph represent. And all those things that scare people? They are the little valleys in between. These little blips scare people. Look at the one in 2009; that was the Great Recession, the biggest percentage drop in the market in 50 years. How does it compare to the giant mountain that followed it? Look at the little downward needle in 2020 – that was the whole impact of Covid-19. You can barely even see that little blip compared to what's happening all around it. In some ways it really is true that a picture is worth a thousand words.

But, what is really on people's minds right now? There are a couple of things. One is that people are wondering about the state of the US economy, what's going to lie ahead. Are we going to go into a recession? When are the rate cuts going to start happening? We had the last rate hike in July of last year, and you've been hearing about a possible rate cut this year. And then, what's the potential impact of the presidential election that's happening? Well, let me tell you one thing about that: it doesn't matter who gets elected President. I don't care who ultimately gets into office because that does not affect the market. In fact, it's the opposite. The market actually affects the presidential election, and I will give you one example of how it does.

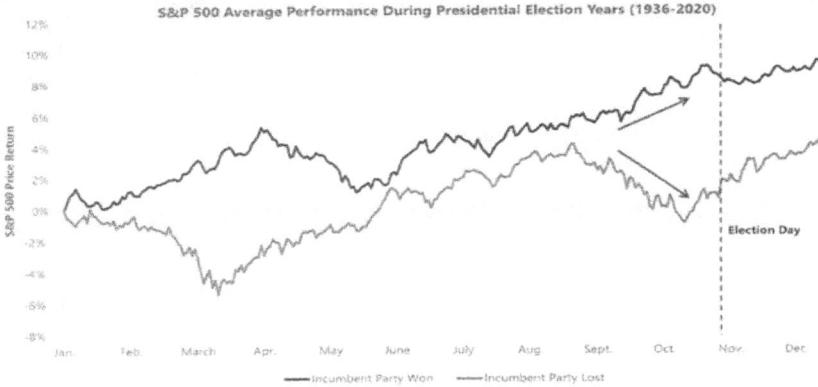

FIG. 12: STOCKS ANTICIPATE ELECTION OUTCOME

So you can see in figure 12, if the market is up that last quarter (Aug - Oct), then whichever party is in office stays. If it's down, whichever party is in office is out. The market has correctly "predicted" every election 82% of the time since 1936.

The Long Term Outlook
for Social Security

Right now, we have 11,200 people a day hitting 65 years old. These are the baby boomers, my generation, and we're the biggest generation in history. As we hit retirement age in such large numbers, we're killing the system. You're hearing about Medicare and Social Security having financial issues. You can see in Figure 13 that we are in a period of peak retirement right now that will continue until the end of the decade. Remember what I said earlier about how we are living too long. When you look at the system right now, you can see that the trust funds actually run out of money in 2035.

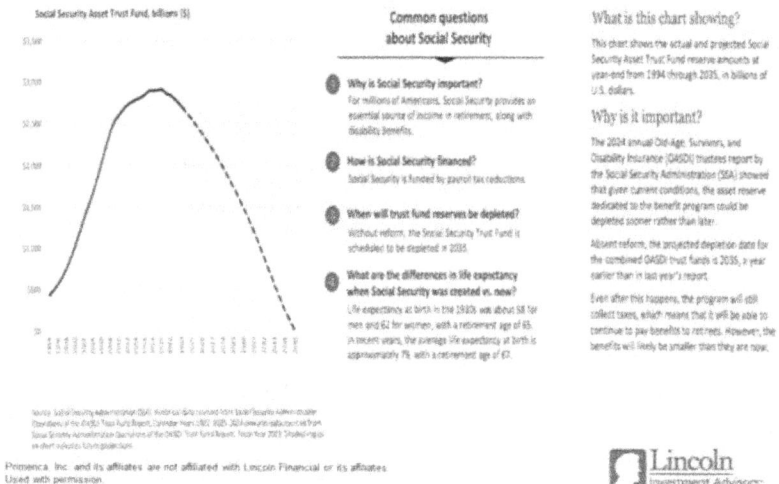

FIG. 13: LONG-TERM OUTLOOK FOR SOCIAL SECURITY

Now, it doesn't mean Social Security is going away. It means the surplus is over. So, if some of these people running for President and Congress don't try to do something different with the system, we are going to be in trouble. What are they going to have to do? They're going to have to raise the age at which you can start collecting benefits, lower the amount of benefits, or tax the crap out of people who are still working. None of those options are very favorable at this point, and if a politician says they want to fix this, it's almost like political suicide. But if nothing changes by 2035, the benefits that you will be receiving will likely be reduced by up to 25%. And it'll get a little bit lower every single year after that. So that becomes a real issue if you are depending on Social Security for your retirement.

So, this is one of the things people fear now, something that makes some of them panic. But if you go back and look at some of the previous times we have had these issues that caused a lot of fear and panic, and you see how the market actually performed, you realize there is no reason to panic. For instance, let's look at the Y2K panic in 1999. Do you remember Y2K? People thought the world was going to come to an end because computers wouldn't be able to click over to the year 2000. They actually thought that planes were going to drop out of the sky. I'll never forget the time one of my clients, a reflexologist in Eastern Pennsylvania, had me come down to her house. She was living in fear about Y2K. She said, "Ron, you got to come down to my basement and see. I'm all prepared." I went down there and thought I was at Costco. She had pallets of water, beans, and other canned goods – it was piled up everywhere. Now we all laugh about it. But it was a real fear back then. Well, look how the market performed. In Figure 14 you can see the drawdown that happened that year – it was minus 12.1%. But look what has happened between then and now. The market is up 248.8%. And you could take any one of these panic attacks that we've had – September 11, the Iraq War, the global financial crisis of 2008 – and look at what has happened to the market since then – unbelievable returns!

Panic Attacks and the S&P 500

Year	Panic Attacks	S&P 500 Max Drawdown	Cumulative 1 Price Ret
1999	Y2K	-12.1%	248.8
2000	Tech Bubble Bursts	-17.2%	191.9
2001	September 11th, 2001 Recession	-29.7%	224.8
2002	Final Tech Bubble Flush, Corporate Scandals (Worldcom)	-33.8%	273.5
2003	Iraq War	-14.1%	387.4
2004	Oil Price Breakout	-8.2%	285.6
2005	Hurricane Katrina	-7.2%	253.8
2006	Fed Culminates Hiking Cycle	-7.7%	243.5
2007	Subprime Cracks Emerge	-10.1%	202.3
2008	Global Financial Crisis, Bank Failures, Auto Bailouts	-48.8%	192.0
2009	Global Financial Crisis Culminates	-27.6%	374.7
2010	European Debt Crisis, Flash Crash	-16.0%	284.5
2011	S&P Downgrades U.S. Debt, Greek Debt Worriedowns	-19.4%	241.0
2012	Euro Crisis, 2nd Greek Bailout	-9.9%	241.0
2013	Taper Tantrum	-5.8%	200.7
2014	Ebola	-7.4%	132.0
2015	Chinese Slowdown, Yuan Devaluation, Deflation Scare	-12.4%	108.3
2016	Brexit, Global Negative Rates	-10.5%	109.8
2017	North Korea Tensions Escalate	-2.8%	91.5
2018	Trade Wars, Short Vol Unwind	-19.8%	60.4
2019	Repo Crisis, Yield Curve Inversion	-6.8%	71.1
2020	Covid-19 Pandemic	-33.9%	32.7
2021	Covid Variants, Chinese Regulatory Crackdown	-5.2%	14.2
2022	Russian Invasion of Ukraine, Fed's Hawkish Pivot	-25.4%	-10.0
2023	Regional Bank Crisis, Debt Ceiling Drama	-10.3%	24.2

FIG. 14: PANIC ATTACKS AND THE S&P 500

But, the one that every reader should be really familiar with is Covid-19 because we just experienced it in 2020. We were on the longest bull run ever, right up to February 19th, when the market hit the all-time high. Then Covid hit. In a matter of 34 days, the market dropped 34%. That was the fastest drop to a bear market we've ever had in history – twice as fast as the Great Depression. On March 23rd, the Wall Street Journal came out with a headline you can see in Figure 15: "Investors Fear Worst Is Yet to Come!" This is a perfect example of how the media spreads fear. Imagine thinking, "I worked 30 years of my life and I just lost a third of my money in a month, and now the Wall Street Journal is saying the worst is yet to come!

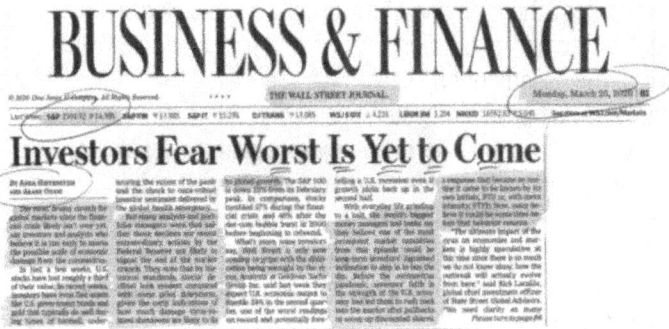

April 2020 (just after this article),was the best
month in the market (12.82%*) in the last 40 years!**

FIG. 15: TUNE OUT THE NOISE

It was one of the single biggest moves out of the market in history. In April of 2020, $866 billion flowed out of the market and went into bank accounts. More money flowed into the banks in a month than in the previous record year. One month later in May, it was another $604 billion. Nobody knew that when this Wall Street Journal article came out in March, we had already hit the bottom of the market, because there is no bell that rings. The very next month, the market returned 12.82% – the best month in the last 40 years!

At the time I said, just for the hell of it I want to see how long it takes the banks to make a trillion-dollar profit on that money by putting it back into the market. So, I tracked it every single month. In that first month of April, when the market returned 12.82%, if the banks put all of that $866 billion in new deposits into the market they would have made $111 billion – in one month! How long did it take the banks to make a trillion dollars? 17 months. That's money that should be in our pockets, not the banks' pockets. If you had $100,000 invested and you just left it alone, in that 17-month period your $100,000 made $79,033. You know what your CD made if you took your money out and put it the bank? $137. Now we're 52 months out, and if you left your $100,000 in the market you have earned $128,727, compared to $11,468 in your CD!

Do you understand why the rich get richer and the poor get poorer?

Consumer Saving & Borrowing

Let's take a closer look at how we got to where we are now. Remember when Covid hit, the government gave out $10 trillion in stimulus money. We went into a recession, but it wasn't a recession that was based on problems in the economy. We put ourselves into a recession because the government shut all the businesses down. The effect was a huge surplus in savings. look at the spike in savings shown in Figure 16 – we started saving almost 16% of our disposable income. We weren't saving because we wanted to, we were saving because we couldn't spend the damn money because the government closed all of the businesses. Everything got crazy at that point. Well, now we're kind of back to normal, and you can see our savings rate right now is at 3.6%.

Consumer Saving and Borrowing

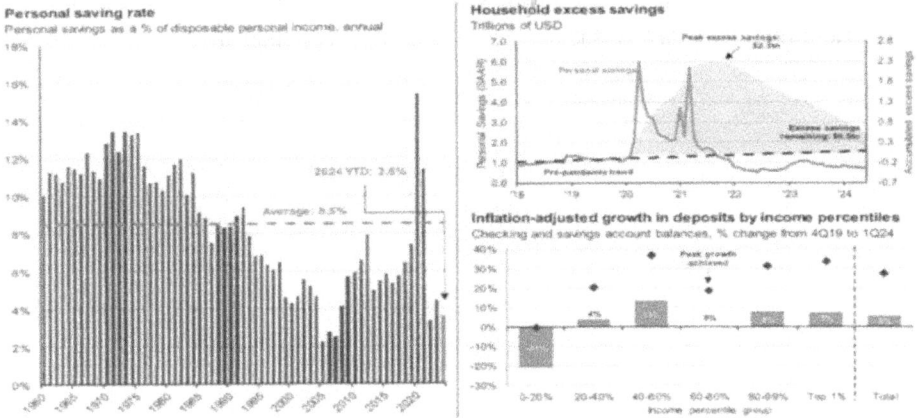

Source: BEA, Federal Reserve, J.P. Morgan Asset Management. (Top right) From March 2020 to August 2021, consumers amassed a peak $2.3 trillion in excess savings relative to the pre-pandemic trend. Since August 2021, consumers have drawn down on those excess savings, with the remaining reflected in the chart annotation. (Bottom right) Deposits include money in checking accounts, savings accounts, CDs and money market deposit accounts. It does not include direct holdings of money market shares. The diamond reflects the peak growth in inflation-adjusted savings achieved during the period and the blue bar reflects current levels.
Guide to the Markets – U.S. Data are as of August 14, 2024.

Finmerica, inc. and its affiliates are not affiliated with J.P. Morgan or its affiliates
Used with permission

J.P.Morgan
ASSET MANAGEMENT

FIG. 16: CONSUMER SAVING & BORROWING

And the $2.3 trillion peak in savings that we hit in 2022 is gone. How are we making up the difference now? We're credit-carding. Credit card debt now is well over a trillion dollars. At an average credit card interest rate of 24.49%. That's nuts. But we're spending money. And corporate earnings are at record highs. Those are the two things that drive the market. Two thirds is consumer spending and one third is corporate earnings both are very, very strong.

Now you're starting to hear that, because of what's happening, the Fed is looking at lowering the rate. The next meeting is September 17th and 18th, and it looks like the Fed will drop the rate at least 25 and possibly 50 basis points. So that should really spur the market. But why did it take so long to get to this point? Why haven't the higher rates slowed the economy more? You kept hearing we're going to go into a big recession, we're going to have a hard landing. Why didn't it happen? First of all, 58% of outstanding mortgages have an interest rate below 4%. So, higher interest rates didn't affect a lot of consumers because their debt was already refinanced at a much lower rate. And then there is corporate debt. Fifty-one percent of the S&P 500 corporate debt won't mature until after 2030. So, they've also got their debt under control. That's why it took a lot longer to get where we want to be – because we did a really good job refinancing at lower rates when the rate was down a couple of years ago.

The last rate hike by the Fed was last July. In Figure 17, you can see what typically happens in the market one year after the last rate hike. The average return of the S&P in the year after a hike is 15.2%. And where are we now, one year after the July 2023 hike? 16% – right on the money. This is exactly what should be happening.

What a Fed Pause Has Meant for Stocks

1-Year Returns Following Last Rate Hike

Last Rate Hike	S&P 500	Russell 1000 Growth	Russell 1000 Value	Russell Mid Cap	Russell 2000
Feb. 1980	15.5%	18.0%	11.5%	21.9%	25.8%
May 1981	-15.5%	-18.4%	-15.2%	-18.3%	-20.5%
Aug. 1984	13.2%	11.7%	16.9%	18.3%	13.1%
Feb. 1989	14.8%	17.6%	9.6%	8.9%	2.1%
Feb. 1995	35.2%	36.6%	33.8%	31.8%	28.0%
May 2000	-12.3%	-30.3%	5.0%	0.6%	-1.8%
June 2006	18.1%	17.3%	18.8%	19.3%	16.7%
Dec. 2018	30.6%	36.9%	24.5%	26.1%	26.1%
Median	**15.2%**	**17.5%**	**14.2%**	**18.8%**	**14.9%**

Worst Performing   Best Performing

▷ Stocks have historically delivered robust returns following the Fed's final rate hike, with large growth and mid cap leading the way.

ClearBridge   Sources: FactSet, Russell, S&P. Month-end dates used to calculate returns through 1990, Jan. 31, 1995 used to calculate the Feb. 1, 1995 pause. Exact last hike dates used from 1995 present. Past performance is not a guarantee of future results. Investors cannot invest directly in an index, and unmanaged index returns do not reflect any fees, expenses or sales charges.

Primerica, Inc. and its affiliates are not affiliated with ClearBridge or its affiliates.
Used with permission.

FIG. 17: ONE-YEAR RETURNS FOLLOWING A FED PAUSE

Inflation

Another big factor that is critical to consider is inflation. Inflation became a major issue because everything was closed down during Covid. If you studied economics in school you learned about supply and demand – if there's more demand than supply, prices go up, and vice versa. So, because people couldn't get things, prices went up, and we hit an all-time high inflation rate during the last 40 years in June 2022 at 9.1%. The truth is, that's nothing compared to what inflation was in the early eighties. But I loved it when people would say to me, "We've never had this kind of inflation!" I guess they were just too young to remember.

I got my first mortgage in 1982 at a rate of 14.5% and I thought I'd died and gone to heaven with a rate like that because interest rates were running at 18-19% back then. So, 9% is not the highest it's ever been. We've been here before. But that was when the Fed started aggressively raising the rate, because the goal is we've got to hurt the consumer. It's sad when we have to do it. We want more people unemployed. We want more of their money going to interest instead of principal, so they can't buy more stuff. And that's why they raised the rate – so that they could start driving down inflation.

Has it worked? It's working picture perfectly In figure 18, you can see inflation was down to 3.1% at the beginning of 2024. Since then, it ticked up slightly but then came back down. And the numbers for July 2024 just came out, and we're at 2.9%. The Fed's goal is 2%, so we're right where we need to be. Federal Reserve Chairman Powell didn't lower the rate in the July 2023 meeting because, although it was going in the right direction, he said he needed to see more. Well, he just saw more.

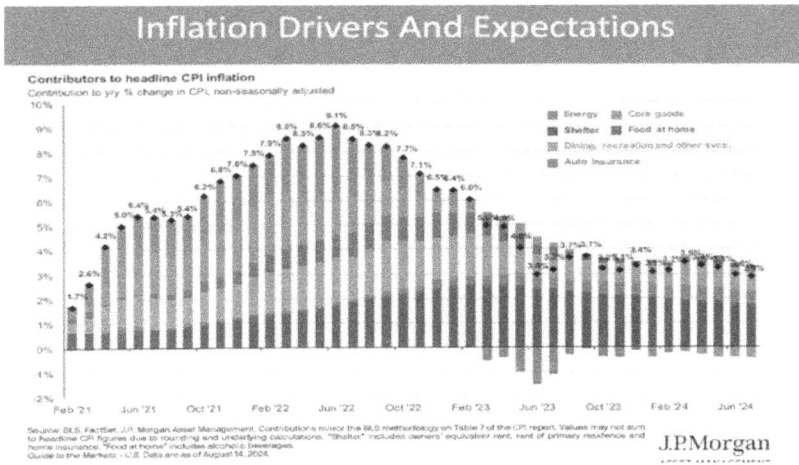

FIG. 18: INFLATION DRIVERS AND EXPECTATIONS

The "Stamp" Story

But, when you look at inflation, here's what I want you to realize. It's natural to have periods of higher and lower inflation. It's not "different this time." I was lucky enough to have mentorship from a guy named Nick Murray. If you want a great book on investing, his book called *Simple Wealth, Inevitable Wealth* is now in its 25th edition. That's how many times he rewrote his book – because people keep saying, "This time it's different." So, he rewrites the whole book to prove it's not different this time. We go through growth, recession, inflation, and we keep repeating that process. That process will keep repeating forever. It's not different. It never is and it never will be. But Nick gave me a postage stamp, and said he would tell me a story about it. And, then I needed to tell this story for the rest of my life. He said, "If you tell this story, you'll create wealth. But if you're going to create wealth and not continually share it till the day you die, then I'm not interested in even getting together with you." So, he gave me that stamp, and he said, "Here's the story."

30-Year Retirement Income Crisis

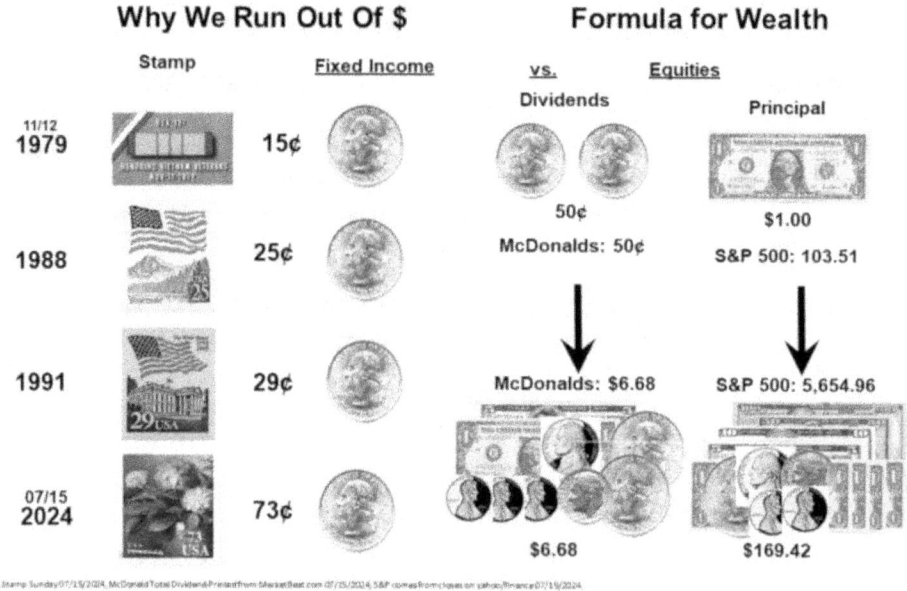

FIG. 19: THE STAMP STORY

The stamp was a 15-cent stamp honoring Vietnam vets. It was dated November 11th, 1979, Veteran's Day. Now, in retirement, most people are on a fixed income. So, let's say in retirement in 1979, you have a quarter coming in, and your only responsibility is you've got to buy a stamp once a year. So, you have 25 cents, and the stamp is 15 cents – that means you have 10 cents left over. You're okay. Everybody's happy. Well, by 1988, that stamp costs 25 cents due to inflation. That's exactly what you have coming in. What if your car breaks down or your roof leaks? You've got a problem because there's nothing left over. By 1991, it's 29 cents for the stamp, and you've got a quarter coming in. What do you do? You're short. People say, "Well, I guess I'd borrow money." No, you've been retired for 12 years. Who's lending you money? You don't have any earned income. You know what you're going to do? Your butt's going back to work, like the majority of people in this country ultimately have to do. And look at where we are now: you can see at the bottom of Figure 19 that stamp is now 73 cents. That's what inflation does. But there is a way to beat inflation, and that is investing in equities.

Investing in Equities

Equity investments provide two ways of making money: dividends and capital appreciation. Let's take a look at dividends first. We'll just take one equity, McDonald's, and go back to 1979. The dividend payout was 50 cents. The dividend payout as of July 15th, 2024, was $6.68. You can see just the dividend alone was enough to pay for that stamp at the price of 73 cents with a bunch of money left over. But, that's not even where the big money is. The big money is the capital appreciation. You can see on the right side of Figure 19 that the S&P closed on November 12th, 1979 at 103.51. On July 15th, 2024 it closed at 5,654.96. That means every dollar you had invested in 1979 is worth $169.42 today. Is that pretty cool? That's why investing in equities is a formula for creating not only wealth, but generational wealth.

The Labor Market

Labor is the other thing that you've been hearing people talk about lately. Right now there are about 1.5 jobs for every one person looking. So that's another little bit of an issue. But, again, unemployment is moving in the right direction. The problem with a labor shortage is it takes labor to make a product. If employees are in demand because there's 1.5 jobs for every one person looking, that means they can demand more money. And, if companies have to pay more for labor, they are going to put that in the price of the products, which keeps inflation up.

But, as you saw on page 33, inflation is coming down. We're on the right track. The unemployment rate was the big thing that really screwed things up. It was at 3.8, then it went to 3.9, then 4.0, then 4.1. For the month of July it jumped to 4.3, and that was the panic that was happening last week. But keep in mind, that is what it was supposed to do. That is what Federal Reserve Chairman Powell was looking for – to make sure we were moving in the right direction before he decides to cut interest rates. Wage growth is also coming down. It is now at 3.8%, exactly where we want it to be.

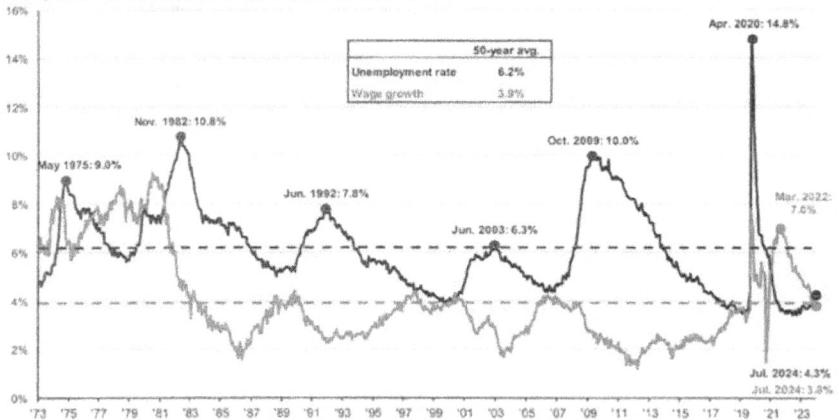

Unemployment & Wages-Drivers Of Economic & Market Resiliency

Civilian unemployment rate and year-over-year wage growth
Private production and non-supervisory workers, seasonally adjusted, percent

	50-year avg.
Unemployment rate	6.2%
Wage growth	3.9%

Apr. 2020: 14.8%
Nov. 1982: 10.8%
May 1975: 9.0%
Oct. 2009: 10.0%
Jun. 1992: 7.8%
Jun. 2003: 6.3%
Mar. 2022: 7.6%
Jul. 2024: 4.3%
Jul. 2024: 3.8%

Source: BLS, FactSet, J.P. Morgan Asset Management. Private production and non-supervisory jobs represent just over 80% of total private nonfarm jobs.
Guide to the Markets – U.S. Data are as of August 14, 2024.

J.P.Morgan
ASSET MANAGEMENT

Presidential Elections

Presidential Approval Ratings and Market Performance

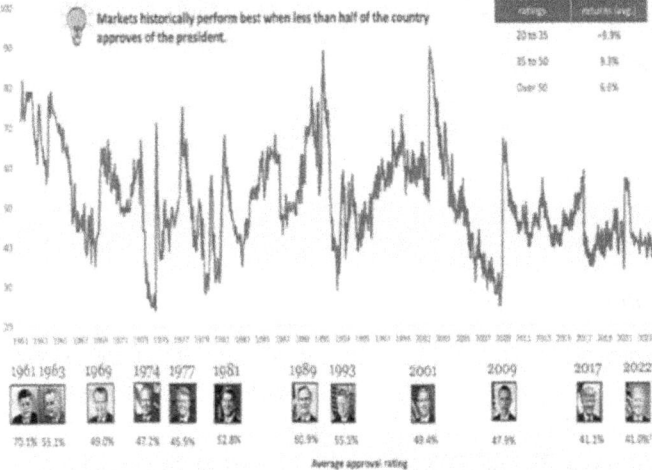

FIG. 20: MODERATE TO LOW PRESIDENTIAL APPROVAL DOES NOT HURT THE MARKET

And then there is the presidential election. Here's the interesting thing about the presidential election. If the President has an approval rating of 35 to 50%, which means a majority of the people don't like the job he's doing, the market has historically done better than when the President has majority approval. It is kind of ridiculous, right? You can see in Figure 20, if their approval rating is 35 to 50 percent, the market actually averages 9.3%, compared to 6.6% when they have approval above 50%. And, this goes all the way back to President Kennedy. So the presidential election has nothing to do with what's going on in the market.

In fact, I want to prove it to you. If you go all the way back to 1926, and you invested $1,000 on January 1st, your money is now worth $14,567,541. And you can see in Figure 21, it doesn't matter which party was in the White House.

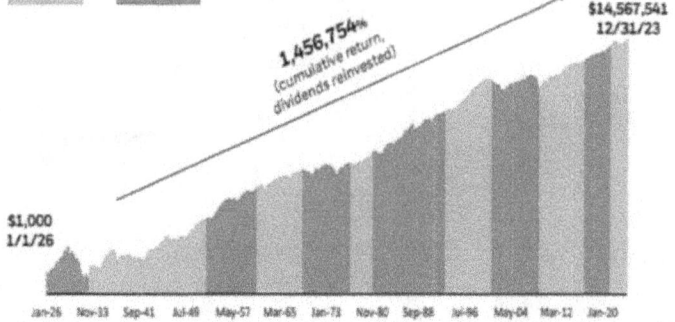

Growth of $1k since 1926

Cumulative returns, 1/1/26 – 12/31/23

FIG. 21: THE MARKET DOESN'T CARE WHICH PARTY IS IN THE WHITE HOUSE

Here are some more interesting things about presidential elections. Election years have historically generated strong returns. Going back to 1928, stocks have had a positive return in 20 of the last 24 election years (83%) with an average 12% return. In all the years during that timeframe, stocks rose 73% of the time, with an overall average return of 11%. Since 1936, the annualized 10-year return on an investment made at the beginning of an election year, as measured by the S&P, was 11.2% when a Democrat won and 10.5% when a Republican won. So it doesn't really matter, market wise. We should all stop thinking that politics matters in the long term. It is the market that influences politics, not the other way around.

Recession Risk

What is a recession? A recession is anytime we have two straight quarters of negative GDP (Gross Domestic Product) growth. Well, according to government statistics, we already had that. The first quarter of 2022 was down 1.6% and the second quarter we were down 0.6%. That's the definition of a recession. Where are we now? We just finished the second quarter of 2024 at 2.8% GDP growth. That's phenomenal. Does it mean we're not in danger of a recession? Well, one way we measure that is with the Clearbridge Recession Risk Dashboard, as shown in figure 22 below.

U. S. Recession Risk Dashboard

- 12 variables have historically foreshadowed a looming recession
- The overall dashboard is currently signaling expansion

		July 31, 2024	March 31, 2024	December 31, 2023
Consumer	Housing Permits	Caution	Caution	Recession
	Job Sentiment	Recession	Recession	Recession
	Jobless Claims	Caution	Caution	Caution
	Retail Sales	Caution	Caution	Caution
	Wage Growth	Expansion	Recession	Recession
Business Activity	Commodities	Caution	Caution	Caution
	ISM New Orders	Caution	Caution	Recession
	Profit Margins	Expansion	Recession	Recession
	Truck Shipments	Caution	Caution	Caution
Financial	Credit Spreads	Expansion	Caution	Caution
	Money Supply	Caution	Recession	Recession
	Yield Curve	Recession	Recession	Recession
	Overall Signal	Expansion	Caution	Recession

Expansion Caution Recession

ClearBridge

Data as of July 31, 2024. Sources: BLS, Federal Reserve, Census Bureau, ISM, BEA, American Chemistry Council, American Trucking Association, Conference Board, Bloomberg, CME, FactSet and Macrobond. The ClearBridge Recession Risk Dashboard was created in January 2016. References to the signals it would have sent in the years prior to January 2016 are based on how the underlying data was reflected in the component indicators at the time.

Primerica, Inc. and its affiliates are not affiliated with ClearBridge Investments or its affiliates
Used with permission.

FIG. 22: RECESSION RISK DASHBOARD

This is a dashboard that comes out every month, and it looks at 12 different indicators that really make up the economics of our country and then gives an overall signal. This dashboard has signaled a recession since August of 2022. You can see in Figure 22, that in late 2023 the overall signal was still showing a recession. It turned around earlier this year and changed to a "caution" signal. And, for the last two months, the signals have been showing we are in an expansion.

So, we are out of recession and into expansion mode right now. And remember, we were technically in a recession last year, according to government numbers. But, look what happens to the market one year after a recession. Figure 23 shows that the average return one year after a recession is 16%. So how did the market actually do the past year? Well, the S&P average one-year return was 26% even higher! And you can see, in Figure 23, that the cumulative average return three years after a recession is 31%, and after five years it's 56%. So, when you look at the market, always remember what I said earlier: it's seven steps forward, one step back. That's the way it is. That's the way it will always be.

Equity Performance Around U. S. Recessions

S&P 500 Index Price Return

Recession Start Date	Duration (Months)	Return During Recession	Return 1 Yr. After Recession	Return 3 Yrs. After Recession	Return 5 Yrs. After Recession
July 1953	10	18%	30%	62%	101%
August 1957	8	-4%	33%	50%	62%
April 1960	10	17%	10%	23%	44%
December 1969	11	-6%	3%	10%	5%
November 1973	16	-13%	23%	7%	22%
January 1980	6	7%	8%	34%	57%
July 1981	16	6%	20%	46%	66%
July 1990	8	1%	8%	19%	72%
March 2001	8	-2%	-5%	3%	23%
December 2007	18	-38%	12%	48%	113%
February 2020	2	-1%	44%	43%	N/A
Average return		-1%	+16%	+31%	+56%
Number of positive periods (%)		45%	91%	100%	100%

What is this chart showing?

This chart shows performance of the S&P 500 Index in the periods during and after past U.S. recessions.

Did you know?

+16%
Average S&P return one year after recession

+31%
Average S&P return three years after recession

+56%
Average S&P return five years after recession

Why is it important?

Although recessions can be a time of uncertainty, investors likely shouldn't let the prospect of a bumpy landing for the economy keep them from staying invested.

History shows that returns during recessionary periods have been relatively mixed, lending itself to the adage that the stock market is not the economy.

Returns following recessions have been strong, with cumulative gains one, three and five years later of 16%, 31%, and 56%.

Additionally, the S&P 500 was negative only one time 12 months following the end of a recession and generated a positive return 100% of the time both three and five years later.

Source: Morningstar, NBER Cumulative price returns of the S&P 500 Index. Past performance does not guarantee future results. Recession durations measured from the first day of the month following the peak month, to the initial low trough month.

LIN-442809.00104   for use with the general public.

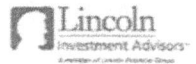

Primerica, Inc. and its affiliates are not affiliated with Lincoln Financial Group or its affiliates. Used with permission

Lincoln
Investment Advisors

FIG. 23: STRONG STOCK PERFORMANCE AFTER RECESSIONS

Bull & Bear Markets

You can think of bull markets as the "seven steps forward", and bear markets as the "one step back." And, the thing about bear markets is, they don't last very long. Let's take a look at one of the worst, the Great Recession, that started on October 9th, 2007 and ended on March 9th, 2009.

S&P 500 Index, cumulative total returns[1]

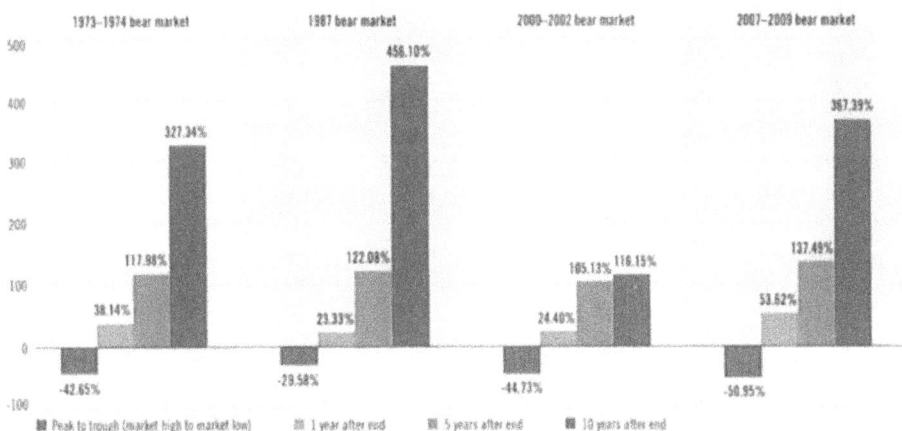

	1973–1974 bear market	1987 bear market	2000–2002 bear market	2007–2009 bear market
Peak to trough (market high to market low)	-42.65%	-29.58%	-44.73%	-50.95%
1 year after end	38.14%	23.33%	24.40%	53.62%
5 years after end	117.98%	122.08%	105.13%	137.49%
10 years after end	327.34%	456.10%	116.15%	367.39%

1. Source: Bloomberg. Past performance is no guarantee of future results. This chart is for illustrative purposes only and is not indicative of performance at any specific investment. All investments involve risks, including loss of principal. Please note that an investor cannot invest directly in an index. Unmanaged index returns do not reflect any fees, expenses or sales charges. This chart illustrates the historical performance of the Standard & Poor's 500 Index (S&P 500) before and after the bear market bottoms of October 3, 1974, December 4, 1987, October 9, 2002 and March 9, 2009. Cumulative total returns include reinvestment of dividends and capital gains. The S&P 500 Index is an unmanaged index of 500 stocks that is generally a representation of the performance of larger companies in the US.

FranklinTempleton.com, Learning from the lessons of time

FIG. 24: MARKET PERFORMANCE IN BEAR MARKETS AND THE FOLLOWING 10 YEARS

You can see on the right side of Figure 23, that the S&P 500 Index dropped 50.95% during that period of 1.4 years. But, then it was over. One year later it's up 53.62%, 5 years later it's up 137.49%, and 10 years later it's up 367.39%. So the key is, don't let your emotion drive your decisions like some people have been doing recently. One thing that you may have heard is that we're moving toward a market correction because the market is down about 8.5% from a month ago. A drop of 10% is considered a market "correction." So people are saying, "Oh my God, we're going to have a correction!" Do you realize that on average we have a correction every year? Going all the way back to 1983, the average intra-year decline is minus 10.1%. That means at some point during the year, the market declined by that much. It's technically a correction happening every year.

Volatility Does Not Equal a Financial Loss Unless You Sell

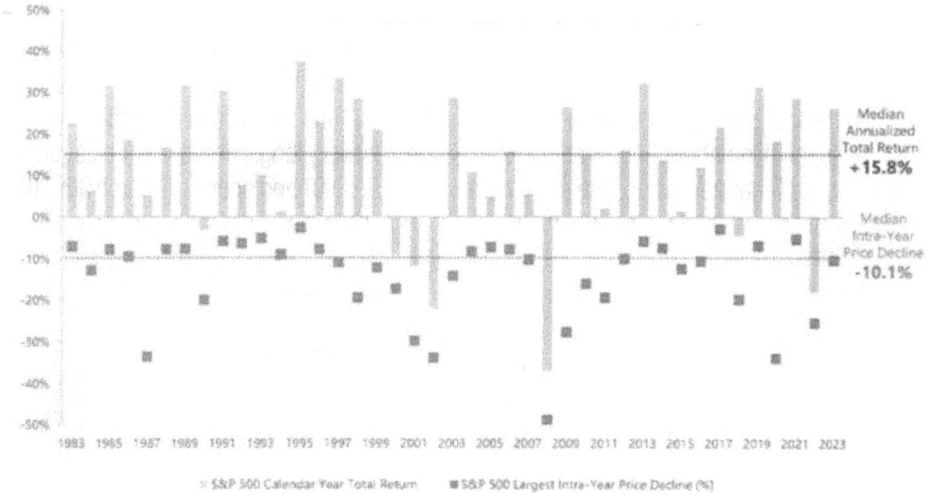

FIG. 25: VOLATILITY IS NOT A LOSS UNLESS YOU SELL

But that is not the end of the story, because the market doesn't finish there. You can see, in Figure 25, that the average annual return since 1983 is 15.8% – that's all those grey bars you see sticking up, with very few going downward. That is the rate of return despite those average intra year drops of 10% – all the dots you see on there. So, if you start understanding that what's going on is normal, you just leave it alone. You let it run its course, because you don't lose money unless you sell.

Another issue right now, is the fact that there is about $6 trillion sitting in money market accounts ready to go in the market. These are big institutions that are trying to time it just right and move their cash into the market when the Fed cuts interest rates. You can see on the left side of Figure 26, that this is one of the highest amounts of cash we have ever had ready to go back into the market. You can see in that graph three previous peaks in money market assets, and, then on the right, you can see what happened to the stock market in the next three years after the peaks: 16.4%, 19.3%, and 12.9% returns, respectively.

Returns Following Money Market Asset Peaks

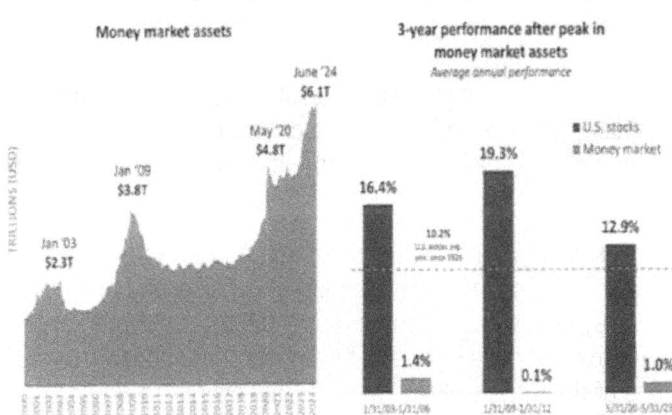

Money market assets

Jan '03
$2.3T

Jan '09
$3.8T

May '20
$4.8T

June '24
$6.1T

TRILLIONS (USD)

3-year performance after peak in money market assets
Average annual performance

■ U.S. stocks
▨ Money market

16.4%

10.2%
U.S. stocks avg. ann. since 1926

1.4%

1/31/03-1/31/06

19.3%

0.1%

1/31/09-1/31/12

12.9%

1.0%

5/31/20-5/31/23

What is this chart showing?

This chart shows the rise in money market assets over time, and how money markets and U.S. stocks performed over the three-year period following peak money market assets.

Why is it important?

While it can be beneficial for investors to hold cash for preservation or liquidity purposes, holding too much can lead to suboptimal results.

Money market fund assets continue to touch new all-time highs.

Historically, this has been a bullish sign for stocks as they have performed better than average following periods of peak money market assets.

Source: Chart (left): Morningstar. Data most recently available as of 7/31/24. Chart (right): Morningstar, Blackrock Student of the Markets, Lincoln Financial Group. Returns calculated from end of peak month listed. US Stocks = S&P 500 TR; Money Market = Morningstar taxable money market category average returns. Past performance does not guarantee or predict future performance.

LCN-6893886-063124

For use with the general public.

Primerica, Inc. and its affiliates are not affiliated with Lincoln Financial Group or its affiliates. Used with permission.

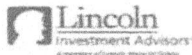

Lincoln
Investment Advisors

FIG. 26: STOCK MARKET RETURNS AFTER MONEY MARKET PEAKS

Can You Time the Market?

You might get the idea from what I've been saying that it's important to time your investments in the market just right. Maybe if you had a crystal ball that would work. But nobody has a crystal ball. What I really want you to understand is that you don't need to time the market.

Let's imagine an investor back in 1945, with $100 and a damn good crystal ball, trying to get the most out of his $100 by investing when the market is rising, and then selling before it starts falling. Let's say he always bought in 12 months after the market hit a low, and sold 12 months prior to reaching a peak, and he did this continuously from 1945 until now. This would be one of the most brilliant investors that ever lived. You can see, in Figure 27, that his hundred dollars is worth $11,167 today. Those flat areas you see in the trendline are where he took his money out.

On the other hand, if you did what I teach our clients to do, if you properly allocated that money in the right equity baskets (I'll get to that shortly), and then you just left it alone and didn't do anything with it, look what happened to your money. Your $100 is worth $41,118. That's almost four times more money. Talk about a big difference. And you don't have to time the market at all.

Growth of $100: Buy & Hold vs. Market Timing Since 1945?

Cumulative Price Return (Log Scale): $100,000 / $10,000 / $1,000 / $100 / $10

Cumulative Return: $41,118

Cumulative Return: $11,167

Years: 1945, 1955, 1965, 1975, 1985, 1995, 2005, 2015

———— Cumulative Return: Buy & Hold   ———— Cumulative Returns: Buy 12 Months After Trough, Sell 12 Months Before Peak

▶ Since 1945, an investor that consistently sold 12 months prior to a market peak and bought back 12 months after the trough was worse off overall than a buy-and-hold investor.

ClearBridge

FIG. 27: TRYING TO TIME THE MARKET

But, let's look at an opposite kind of example. If you're timing the market, it means you want to buy low and sell high, right? Well, let's say you're someone with terrible luck. Every year you put $1,000 into the market, but somehow every year you managed to buy in at the high point of the year, going back all the way to 1950. You'd have to have impossibly bad luck to do that! But even if you did, right now your account is worth $2,795,487, compared to having $448,824 if you had put the same money into CDs (see Figure 28). You're way ahead of the game.

Value of $1,000 Invested Each Year

$2,795,487

$448,824

At the S&P 500 High Each Year — In T-Bills on Jan. 1 Each Year

▶ Even if an investor were to methodically put money to work at the annual high water mark in equities, they would still have outperformed T-Bills handily since 1950.

▶ There is validity to the old adage "it's not timing the market, it's time in the market".

ClearBridge

Note: Price Return. Data as of Dec. 31, 2023. Sources: FactSet, Federal Reserve, S&P. Past performance is not a guarantee of future results. Investors cannot invest directly in an index, and unmanaged index returns do not reflect any fees, expenses or sales charges.

Primerica, Inc. and its affiliates are not affiliated with Clearbridge or its affiliates. Used with permission

FIG. 28: TIME IS ON YOUR SIDE

The purpose of all this is to let you know it's a long-term approach. The period of time you see in that last graph includes a lot of market shocks: we had an energy crisis back in the seventies – remember that? We had Black Monday. We had the tech bubble and the global financial crisis in 2008. And yet, if you had $10,000 in the market in 1974, 50 years ago, and you just left it there, your account is $3,166,147 now. The only question about timing that is important is: how quickly can I get my money in the market and working for me?

The Cost of Procrastination

I want to drive home how much procrastination hurts you in the market. I've said you should always pay yourself first, meaning put away money for your future before you take care of anything else. What happens if you don't get it done, if you pay yourself last and not first? Let's imagine two investors putting their money into the market with an average annual return of 9%. Investor A gets started early and puts away $6,500 a year from the age of 22 to 30. But then he stops – never puts away another dime after that until he retires at age 67. So he invested for 8 years, a total of $52,000. When he retires, his account is worth $2,399,420. Now, investor B doesn't put any money away before the age of 30. His mindset is: I've got plenty of time. I want to get a car, I want a nice house. I'll get around to it soon enough. So he doesn't do anything for the first eight years and then he puts away $6,500 a year every single year from age 30 to 67. He has invested almost five times more money than investor A ($247,000), but he ends up with less when he retires. He's got $2,211,730 compared to $2,399,420 for investor A, even though he invested regularly for 37 years and investor A for only 8 years. Doesn't that blow your mind? That's the importance of getting started early.

Investor A

Age	Annual Contribution	End of Year Accumulation
22	$ 6,500	$ 7,110
23	6,500	14,890
24	6,500	23,390
25	6,500	32,700
26	6,500	42,870
27	6,500	54,010
28	6,500	66,180
29	6,500	79,500
30	0	86,960
31	0	95,110
32	0	104,040
33	0	113,800
34	0	124,470
35	0	136,150
36	0	148,920
37	0	162,890
38	0	178,170
39	0	194,880
40	0	213,160
41	0	233,160
42	0	255,030
43	0	278,950
44	0	305,120
45	0	333,740
46	0	365,050
47	0	399,300
48	0	436,750
49	0	477,720
50	0	522,540
51	0	571,550
52	0	625,170
53	0	683,810
54	0	747,960
55	0	818,120
56	0	894,870
57	0	978,810
58	0	1,070,630
59	0	1,171,070
60	0	1,280,920
61	0	1,401,080
62	0	1,532,510
63	0	1,676,270
64	0	1,833,520
65	0	2,005,510
66	0	2,193,650
67	0	2,399,420

Total Contributions: **$52,000**
Total Accumulation at Age 67: **$2,399,420**

Investor B

Age	Annual Contribution	End of Year Accumulation
22	0	0
23	0	0
24	0	0
25	0	0
26	0	0
27	0	0
28	0	0
29	0	0
30	$ 6,500	$ 7,110
31	6,500	14,890
32	6,500	23,390
33	6,500	32,700
34	6,500	42,870
35	6,500	54,010
36	6,500	66,180
37	6,500	79,500
38	6,500	94,070
39	6,500	110,000
40	6,500	127,430
41	6,500	146,490
42	6,500	167,340
43	6,500	190,150
44	6,500	215,100
45	6,500	242,390
46	6,500	272,230
47	6,500	304,880
48	6,500	340,590
49	6,500	379,650
50	6,500	422,370
51	6,500	469,100
52	6,500	520,220
53	6,500	576,130
54	6,500	637,280
55	6,500	704,180
56	6,500	777,340
57	6,500	857,370
58	6,500	944,910
59	6,500	1,040,660
60	6,500	1,145,390
61	6,500	1,259,940
62	6,500	1,385,240
63	6,500	1,522,300
64	6,500	1,672,210
65	6,500	1,836,190
66	6,500	2,015,540
67	6,500	2,211,730

Total Contributions: **$247,000**
Total Accumulation at Age 67: **$2,211,730**

FIG. 29: THE TIME VALUE OF MONEY

Remember I said earlier that you need to have a $1 million in your retirement account by age 65. If you start saving for that when you're age 25, you have to put $381 a month away (based on an average annual return of 7%) to get the job done. If you waited, like many people do, until you're age 55, it's $5,778 a month to get the same job done. Well, that's where it becomes impossible for most people to do it – and that's why they don't get the job done.

Where Most People Are Putting Their Money

Banks

Banks are the number one place where people are keeping their money. And, if you're keeping your money in the bank, you don't have a chance. If you put away $10,000 in the bank with a 1% return, after taxes and inflation (3% right now), the purchasing power of your $10,000 is $9,782 after a year. You're actually losing money. It's crazy.

Life Insurance

Here's the second place people are putting their money: cash value life insurance, the biggest screw job on the planet. Let me tell you how it works. If you have a cash value policy, and this is what most people have, you're paying about $23.01 in premiums per $1,000 of coverage. If you bought term insurance, for the same thousand dollars of coverage, you would've paid $2.07 in premiums. Now, why would anybody pay 11 times more money for the same amount of protection? Well, you must be thinking that there's some type of benefit that you're going to receive if you pay $23 instead of $2, right? That's what people think, but it's not true.

Here are seven reasons why you should never own cash value life insurance.

1. **You lose your cash value when you die**. Let's say you bought a $100,000 life insurance policy at age 35, and your premium is $1,478. You figure that because you paid 11 times more for that policy than you would for a term policy, you're going to have some cash value built up, right? That's what they're selling you. Well, by the time you're age 55, that cash value is $21,737. But, there's something you have to do in order to get paid, and it's not my favorite thing to do. You have to die. It doesn't pay any other way. So, if you die at age 55, you've got $100,000 worth of coverage, and because you paid all that extra premium, you amassed $21,737 worth of cash value. When you die, what does your family get paid? You might think, well, I get $121,737 – my coverage amount plus my savings. Wrong! The bottom line is, you lose your cash value if you die. The only payout would be the coverage amount. By the way, they don't hide that fact. They tell you three places in your contract that you'll lose your cash if you die. One of them is on the cover page at the bottom, written in bold print saying, "The insurance is payable upon death", NOT the insurance and cash value. Now, you have a better chance of dying at age 65. Let's say you pass away at age 65. Your cash value is now $38,000. What does your family get?

A $100,000. How much of that is your own money? $38,000. You see, the longer you own that crap, the more you become your own insurance company. And, that defeats the purpose of buying life insurance in the first place, which is to take the risk off of your family and put it on them.

2. **Delayed savings.** Typically, the first two to five years, you may not accumulate any cash value, even though you paid 11 times more for it. Why? Because that money goes to pay big fat commissions to the guys who sell these policies. You may even have a negative return on your investment after 5 years. In comparison, I would've doubled your money in six years at a 12% market return. Big difference, right?

3. **It costs you to borrow money from your cash value.** Let's go back to the example from number 1. You're 55 years old and you have $21,000 in accumulated cash value. Let's say Covid hits and all of a sudden you need money. How do you get it? Well, your insurance agent will be there pretty quick. He'll come right over to the house. The reason is, they are going to charge you 8% interest to borrow your own money. It doesn't make any sense whatsoever to pay to use your own money, but anyone who has taken a policy loan has done exactly that. If you were paying $1,478 for $100,000 in coverage, now you borrowed $21,000 and have to pay 8% on that, you're now paying them $3,158. And the crazy thing is, you don't have $100,000 in coverage anymore because they will deduct the loan amount from the payout, meaning that your coverage amount has dropped to $79,000.

4. **No life insurance policy qualifies as an IRA.** All the money that goes into cash value life insurance is an after-tax contribution. If you would've bought term life and invested the difference in an IRA, you could have written that difference off your taxes. So, instead of $23 in premiums per $1,000 in coverage, we pay $2, and that means we have $21 that we could have put away in our IRA account. And, we can assume we'll get a quarter of that back in tax savings (which would be $5) because the IRS says if you put money into an IRA in 2024, you can write off up to $7,000 ($8,000 if you're over 50). Double that if you're married. You don't get that tax write-off from cash value life insurance (its kinda like your life insurance was paid by the IRS with $3 left over).

5. **Insurance companies, by law, can hold your cash.** Here's what your policy says: "We have the right to defer making a loan on this or any other contract with us unless the loan would be used to pay premiums to us." So, as long as you're borrowing the money to pay their premiums, they won't make you wait six months to get the money when you request it. But if you have an emergency, when do you need the money? You need it now!

6. **Insurance dividends are *not* dividends.** The life insurance industry is an industry that's largely exempt from truth in lending or full disclosure regulations. So they can tell you, "Oh, you're going to make 5% on your money." And then after five years you're actually at a minus return because of their front-end fees. In my business, if we tell you what you're going to make, you better make that or we're liable.

They use words that we know as investors, like "dividend." We understand that a dividend is a profit – you made money on your money. Well, that's not what an insurance "dividend" is. The US Treasury Department had to come out with a ruling to clarify what an insurance dividend actually is. Treasury Decision 1743 explains that insurance dividends "are simply refunds to the policy holder of a portion of the overcharge collected." So they overcharge you and use your money, and then give you back some of the overcharge which they call a dividend. Really it's just a return of your overcharged money. And, that's why you don't have to pay taxes on it – because you already paid tax on that money. It was an after-tax contribution. But they get to say things that we understand to mean one thing, when they mean something totally different.

7. **Universal life insurance has all the same problems of a cash value policy.** Universal Life insurance policies, as a type of cash value policy, come with several drawbacks similar to those of other cash value policies. One key issue is that the policyholder pays higher premiums than for the same amount of term life insurance, with the excess being "invested" to build cash value. However, the returns on these investments don't meet expectations offered in the "illustration" provided by the sales representative when they sell you the policy. This leads to less cash accumulation than anticipated. Additionally, fees and administrative costs can eat into the cash value, reducing its growth. Market fluctuations can also affect the policy's value, especially if the investments within the policy perform poorly. Finally, Universal Life policies typically require ongoing premium payments, and failing to maintain these payments could cause the policy to lapse, resulting in loss of coverage and the built-up cash value.

Mortgages

Now we're going to look at the third place people put their money: mortgages. And that means we have to talk about how we should think about debt. Most of us spend our whole lives trying to spin three plates. One, you want to be properly protected because one out of three people don't make it to retirement. They die too soon. Two, you want to be financially independent, meaning you can maintain your standard of living without working. And three, you want to be debt-free. But there's good debt and bad debt.

Right now, I see so many people trying to get out of debt. And I know debt's an emotional issue, but you have to make sure that you're covering all three plates. If you just focus on one plate, getting out of debt, and you do it at the expense the other two, guess what's going to happen to you? You're automatically going back into debt. You're not solving your problem at all.

One mistake people make trying to get out of debt is to take a 15-year mortgage instead of a 30-year mortgage. Or, they'll make biweekly mortgage payments instead of monthly, or add extra to pay down the principal. But, when you put this extra money into your mortgage, what is that money actually doing for you?

Let's say you had a dollar and you applied that to the mortgage. Let's also say your mortgage rate is at 5% (which is tax deductible), and you're in the 24% income tax bracket (that's the middle bracket). You can see your net return of that dollar investment was 3.8%, which is not a very exciting return of investment.   Out of curiosity, I asked Dawn, who is our resident accountant, "How many clients do you have?" She responded, "500 clients." "How many of them contribute to a traditional IRA account?" "Probably about 3%." That means 97% of the clients that she has are not putting money away in a traditional IRA account where the IRS allows you to write off $7,000 ($8,000 if you're over 50), and double that if you're married.

If you're in a 24% tax bracket, it means that if you invested that dollar in an IRA vs. paying down your mortgage, you just made a 24% return. I talk about 12% returns a lot, and people ask me, "Where do I make 12%?" Well, right there with that tax write-off, you're guaranteed 24% by the federal government. And then, if you put that money in your IRA instead of giving it to the mortgage company or adding extra principle, and you make just 9% (over the last 50 years the average was 12%), look what happens. Now your return is 33%. So, would you rather make 33% or 3.8%? Take your time. It could be a trick question.

Money Doesn't Care Who Owns It

5% Mortgage Rate
-24% Tax Deductible Interest

9% Investment Return
+24% IRA

= 3.8% Return

= 33% Return

The following information and illustration is not an offer of any mortgage or related services. It is intended as a comparison of the potential benefit of an investment in equity securities versus allocating available funds to a higher mortgage payment.
The potential benefit illustrated would be reduced or not obtained if the investment performed below the assumed 9% annual rate of growth.

Bankrate.com-30 year mortgage rate 5.00 as of May 19,2022

FIG. 30: MONEY DOESN'T CARE WHO OWNS IT

I just refinanced my home three years ago at age 65 and I did it for 30 years. That means I'm going to be making mortgage payments until I'm 95, right? That's not the way to think about it. The term of the mortgage just sets the payment. Who actually pays on a 30-year mortgage for the full 30 years? The average person refinances about every 5-8 years. But the key is you want your money working for you, not for the bank. Remember, this is about creating wealth, and that's what wealthy people do – they leverage their assets to make money. So, if you had a $200,000 loan at 5%, and you took it for 15 years, your payment is $1,581 a month. If you took it for 30 years, your payment is $1,073 a month. That's a difference of $508 a month.

30-Year vs. 15-Year Mortgage
Invest The Difference

Loan Amount: $200,000
Interest: 5%

$1,581	**15 Year Loan Payment**
$1,073	**30 Year Loan Payment**
$ 508	**Difference Per Month**

If You Invested That $508 / Month For 15 Years @ 9% You Would Have:

$193,672	**Amount In Investment @ 15 yrs**
$135,768	**30 yr. Mortgage Balance After 15 yrs.**
$ 57,904	**Left Over After Paying Mortgage Off**

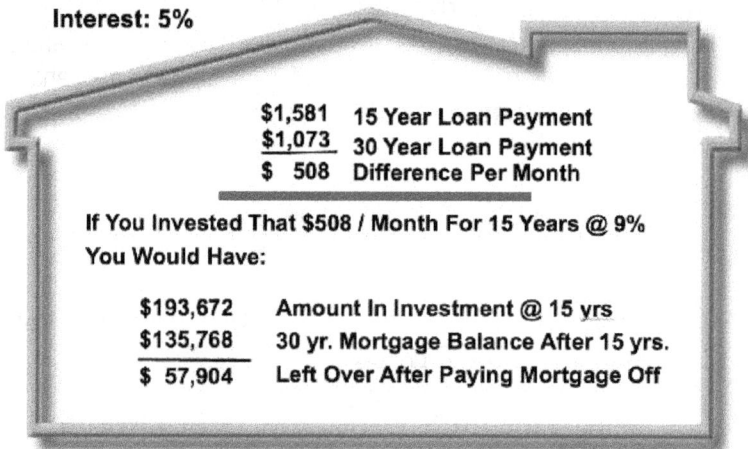

Bankrate.com-30 year mortgage rate 5.00 as of May 19.2022

FIG. 31: 30-YEAR VS. 15-YEAR MORTGAGE

Let's say you made 15 years of on-time payments on your 15-year mortgage. At the end of 15 years you owe nothing. You have no debt. That's good, right? On the other hand, at the end of 15 years I still owe $135,768 on that $200,000 loan, because I took a 30-year mortgage. You look at that and you say, "My house is paid off and you're going to end up paying 2 - 3 times more for yours." And I say, "But the difference is, I took the $508 I saved on my monthly payment, and I put it in an account where I'm making 9% – at the end of 15 years, I've got $193,672 in savings. Now, if I want to, I can just pay off my house, and I'll be almost $60,000 ahead. If you do this calculation based on a 12% return, which is what I always talk about, that's $120,000. The money I made doing my mortgage this way basically covered almost two thirds of the cost of my house!"

Time Scale & Risk

So why don't people do this? One reason is people think the market is risky. They feel like paying down debt is smart and safe, but putting that money in the market is a risk. But, the fact is, on the time scale we're talking about with a mortgage, the market is not a risk.

If someone gave me some money to invest for them and they said they only have a one-year time horizon before they need that money for something important, like buying a car or putting a down payment on a house, I would never put it in the market – not for one year. That's because if you look at the market over one-year holding periods, the market's up 73% of the time and down 27% of the time. That means you have a 27% chance of losing money, and, if you're just looking at a one-year period, that's too much risk. But, look at it over five-year holding periods: it's up 87% of the time and down 13%. More importantly, look at 15-year time periods, which is the time scale we're talking about with mortgages. There has never been a 15-year down period in the market in history.

Does that make sense? But the unfortunate fact is, over the last 20 years the average investor has made no money. This is really sad to me. The market averaged 9.8% over that period. Meanwhile, the average investor earned 3.1%. Why? Because maybe they had a mixture of stocks and bonds, or maybe they were in and out of the market, or all the things that people shouldn't do. But they earned a 3.1% return. What was inflation during that time? 2.5%. And they have to pay tax on that 3.1%. So, if they happened to lose a point off to taxes that 3.1%, they're down to 2.1%, and inflation was 2.5%. They're actually in the hole. If they would've just stayed fully invested in the market, their $10,000 is worth $64,844.

If they missed the 10 best days of the last 20 years for whatever reason – they got in late, they took it out, they were trying to time it, whatever – they gave up half the money they could have earned ($29,708). If they missed the best *40* days of the last 20 years, they actually have a negative return. Their $10,000 is only worth $8,048 now. Pretty ridiculous, right? And here's the interesting part. Seven of the 10 best days occurred within two weeks of the 10 worst days. Do you think you could get in and get out in that short period of time? No, you can't. If you try, you're going to miss it.

Living Off Your Retirement Savings

You've put away your nest egg and now you're in retirement and you want to live off the money. What is that going to look like for you? More specifically, how much can you safely withdraw each year? There is a rule of thumb we call the "4% rule." The idea is, if you don't take more than 4% of your money out each year, you should be okay. Well, here's what these experts say. Bill Bengen says if you diversify among large and small cap stocks, along with some fixed-income assets, you can safely withdraw about 4.5%. Deena Katz, former CEO of Evensky & Katz, says that 4% has been a useful guideline, but 3% is now more realistic. Wade Pfau, professor of retirement income and author, says if you rely on a fixed income like most people do, you can only safely withdraw 2.5%.

How Much Can You Safely Withdraw Each Year?

If you diversify among large- and small-cap stocks and fixed income, the initial "safe" withdrawal rate rises to 4.5 percent.
—Bill Bengen, financial planner

Four percent has been a useful guideline, but it can't be the rule for everyone. Three percent is now a more realistic number.
—Deena Katz, CFP, Evensky & Katz

Those who rely entirely on fixed income can safely withdraw no more than 2.5 percent in the first year, plus inflation increases.
—Wade Pfau, professor of retirement income, American College

AARP Bulletin / Real Possibilities SEPTEMBER 2014

Primerica has not independently verified the facts and statistics attributed to third party sources

FIG. 32: HOW MUCH CAN YOU SAFELY WITHDRAW FROM YOUR NEST EGG EACH YEAR?

Think about what Wade says. If you have a $1 million invested in fixed-income, you can safely live on $2,000 a month (that's what 2.5% of $1 million annually works out to per month). Who can live on $2,000 a month? And by the way, to live on $2,000 a month, it takes $1 million in your retirement account. And what does the average person have in their retirement account right now? $84,714. Nowhere near where we need to be.

A lot of people tell me, "My fear is, what if I retire at the wrong time?" And the answer is, if you understand the rules, there is no wrong time to retire. But let me give you an example. What if you retire, and just your luck, the very next year is one of these major drops in the market that happens once in a generation. We had it in the Great Depression. We had it in 1973-74 (-13.53% and -26.21%, respectively). Remember that, with the gas lines? That was a bad time to retire. Then we had 2001 and 2002 (-12.20% and -22.04%, respectively). So let's say you retired in 1973, a terrible year to retire. Remember we said you're probably going to live in retirement for 30 years. In this case, your 30-year retirement includes not just one, but two once-in-a-generation drops in the market. How does that work out for you? Let's say you have $1,000,000 in 1973 when you retire, and you're taking 6% of the money out per year – not 4%, not 5%, but 6%. So, that's too much according to the rule, but let's talk about 6%.

30-Year Retirement   Jan 73-Dec 03
Withdrawal 6%---Increase 3% per Year

Investment Detail

Period		Beginning Balance	New Investment	Distribution/ Withdrawal	Total Reinvest	Charges & Fees	Taxes Due	Market Value	Net Total Return %
Totals		0	1,000,000	3,000,161	0	0	0	1,058,449	8.72
January-December	1973	0	1,000,000	60,000	0	0	0	812,160	-13.53
January-December	1974	812,160	0	61,800	0	0	0	551,402	-26.21
January-December	1975	551,402	0	63,654	0	0	0	683,828	39.25
January-December	1976	683,828	0	65,564	0	0	0	774,399	24.78
January-December	1977	774,399	0	67,531	0	0	0	651,942	-7.65
January-December	1978	651,942	0	69,556	0	0	0	614,510	5.41
January-December	1979	614,510	0	71,643	0	0	0	644,797	18.36
January-December	1980	644,797	0	73,792	0	0	0	762,318	32.73
January-December	1981	762,318	0	76,006	0	0	0	650,656	-5.11
January-December	1982	650,656	0	78,286	0	0	0	688,728	19.86
January-December	1983	688,728	0	80,635	0	0	0	750,928	22.95
January-December	1984	750,928	0	83,054	0	0	0	706,041	5.60
January-December	1985	706,041	0	85,546	0	0	0	826,769	32.43
January-December	1986	826,769	0	88,112	0	0	0	884,340	19.32
January-December	1987	864,340	0	90,755	0	0	0	849,789	6.95
January-December	1988	849,789	0	93,478	0	0	0	890,980	17.43
January-December	1989	890,980	0	96,282	0	0	0	1,052,140	31.70
January-December	1990	1,052,140	0	99,171	0	0	0	917,781	-3.63
January-December	1991	917,781	0	102,146	0	0	0	1,078,209	31.48
January-December	1992	1,078,209	0	105,210	0	0	0	1,046,460	7.41
January-December	1993	1,046,460	0	108,367	0	0	0	1,035,271	10.16
January-December	1994	1,035,221	0	111,618	0	0	0	936,466	1.37
January-December	1995	936,466	0	114,966	0	0	0	1,139,982	37.79
January-December	1996	1,139,982	0	118,415	0	0	0	1,262,706	23.08
January-December	1997	1,262,706	0	121,968	0	0	0	1,531,416	33.65
January-December	1998	1,531,416	0	125,827	0	0	0	1,820,059	29.80
January-December	1999	1,820,059	0	129,395	0	0	0	2,047,870	20.86
January-December	2000	2,047,870	0	133,277	0	0	0	1,731,411	-9.46
January-December	2001	1,731,411	0	137,276	0	0	0	1,397,083	-12.20
January-December	2002	1,397,083	0	141,394	0	0	0	974,346	-22.04
January-December	2003	974,346	0	145,636	0	0	0	1,058,449	26.88

FIG. 33: A 30-YEAR RETIREMENT EXAMPLE

So you took $60,000 the first year, and in the second year it rose to $61,800 to account for inflation. Each year it rises 3% due to inflation (you can see this in the "Distribution/Withdrawal" column of Figure 33). But because we retired at a bad time, we hit the major drop in market valuation. At the end of the second year, despite having only withdrawn $121,800, you only have $551,402 of your $1,000,000 left (see "Market Value" column). And you say, "Holy crap, I'm in retirement for two years and half my money is already gone!" What do you think the average person would do? Most people would take the money out. Operating on emotion, they would say, "I can't afford to lose any more money. I have to get the money out." And they would've made the biggest mistake of their life.

Let's jump to the end. Let's say you left your money in the market and kept on withdrawing 6% a year for 30 years. In that 30-year period, you withdrew $3,000,161. That's three times more than the $1,000,000 you put in. You weathered two big market drops. What is your account worth at the end of 2003? Your account is worth $1,058,449 (bottom of "Market Value" column). You didn't even touch your principal in 30 years after retiring at the worst possible time!

A Real-Life Example

Are you still skeptical? Maybe you're thinking anybody can make nice hypotheticals, but show me a real-life client. Show me what one of your clients actually experienced. And this is when I talk about my mom and dad. Of all the things I've done in this business over the years, the thing I'm probably most proud of is what I was able to do for my mom and dad. I mentioned earlier that my parents owned a KOA campground. My parents brought the first ones to the East Coast back in the late sixties. For years, I told my dad, "You need to start saving money for retirement." Here's what my dad said: "I don't need to save for retirement. When I'm ready to retire I'll sell the business. That will be my retirement." Famous last words. I said, "Bad idea." So, at age 57 my dad decides to sell the business and he wants $600,000 for it. He can't get it. The business doesn't generate enough revenue to warrant anybody buying it for $600,000. So he sells it to my sister on a long-term agreement of sale, 20 years. Twelve years into it – my dad was 69 years old at the time – we're at one of our family reunions and my dad declares, "I hope I'm dead in eight years. I won't have any money left." (My dad was never the most positive individual on the planet.)

So the first thing I said to my sister was, "Do you want to take care of him the rest of his life?" And she said, hell no. I said, me neither, but you owe him money. So we came up with a plan. My sister would go to the bank and get a mortgage on the place. Then she'd use the money to pay him what she owed in a lump sum, discounted by $50,000. But I would invest that money on his behalf. At the time, my mom and dad were living in the farmhouse in the middle of the camp. We would move them into one of the lodges on the hill, knock the farmhouse down, and put seven more campsites in there. Just the revenue from the seven campsites would be enough to pay the mortgage. So, I invested $245,323.09 for my parents. And that went in on August 5, 2002.

And guess what happened? Just my luck, that was the year the market went down 22.04%. And my parents were withdrawing 7% a year – way too much. I've said the market goes seven steps forward, one step back. Well, they took their one step back right out of the gate. And then six years later, the Great Recession of 2008 hits. That's never happened to anyone from George Washington to my dad. But that's what happened.

My parents now have been retired exactly 22 years. So far, they have withdrawn $316,500 from an initial investment of $245,000. That means they took out all their money plus 29% more. And, their account value today is $327,753.11. They still have 34% more money than they started with 20 years ago. That's no hypothetical. That's my parents' retirement and the thing I'm most proud of. In a way, my parents' story encapsulates everything I try to teach people.

But, returning to the question of how much you can safely withdraw from your retirement account per year, in Figure 34 you can see the probability of meeting your income needs over a 25-year retirement based on the percentage of your retirement you withdraw every year. What you can see is that *how* you invest your money makes all the difference in the world. This is a really big one to understand.

Probability Of Meeting Income Needs

Various Withdrawal Rates and Portfolio Allocations Over a 25-year Retirement

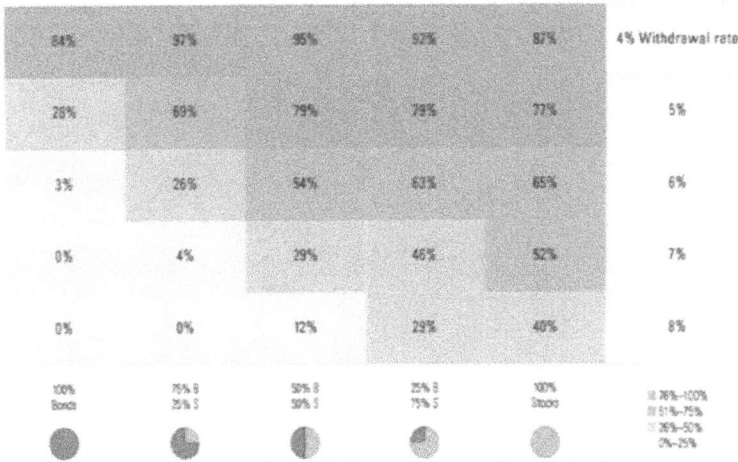

100% Bonds	75% B 25% S	50% B 50% S	25% B 75% S	100% Stocks	
84%	97%	95%	92%	87%	4% Withdrawal rate
28%	69%	79%	79%	77%	5%
3%	26%	54%	62%	65%	6%
0%	4%	29%	46%	52%	7%
0%	0%	12%	29%	40%	8%

FIG. 34: CHANCE OF MEETING INCOME NEEDS WITH DIFFERENT PORTFOLIO MIXES & WITHDRAWAL RATES

At the top of the chart you see a 4% withdrawal rate. That's the rule of thumb, so let's start there. Let's say you're all in bonds. That's the left side of the chart. You've got an 84% chance of lasting 25 years. If you're all in equities, which is the right side of the chart, your chance is 87%. But we know that people are withdrawing way more than 4%. If you're withdrawing 5%, look what happens if you're fully invested in bonds: you now have a 28% chance of making it through your retirement, compared to 77% if you're fully in equities. What if you're withdrawing 6% a year? At 6%, you have a 3% chance of making it if you're all in bonds, a 65% chance if you're in equities. Which situation would you rather be in? But what they tell you is, you're in retirement now and this is the time that you don't want to be in "risky" assets. Ask yourself what the real risk is. The biggest risk would be putting your money in assets like CDs where you're guaranteed to lose money most years. The next biggest risk would be bonds, where you have little chance of making it through your retirement.

This is the thing: While you were working and making money, your assets were also at work making money for you. Now you've decided to retire, which means you're not making money anymore. Why would you want your money to retire too? It's the only thing you've got making money anymore. Now is when you need that money to work the hardest it's ever worked. But that's not the advice you usually hear. Imagine my parents, who were withdrawing 7% a year. What if they had listened to any other advisor saying, "Well, you don't want to be in the market. It's too risky." What is the chance they would have lasted a 25-year retirement if their money was not in the market? Zero. And according to Figure 34, they have a 52% chance of meeting their income needs if their money is fully in the market. You've seen the actual numbers – after 22 years, they've totally beat the odds.

The Nine Baskets

Now I'm going to show you the nine baskets of equities that I mentioned earlier. But first, let's recall that the market has two ways of making money: dividends and capital appreciation. When you look at the market's average return of 11.2% since 1950, 3.3% came from dividends and 7.9% came from capital appreciation. So in order to maximize the market, you need both. And the best way to ensure that you're getting the best of both worlds, is to diversify among the nine different baskets you can see in Figure 35.

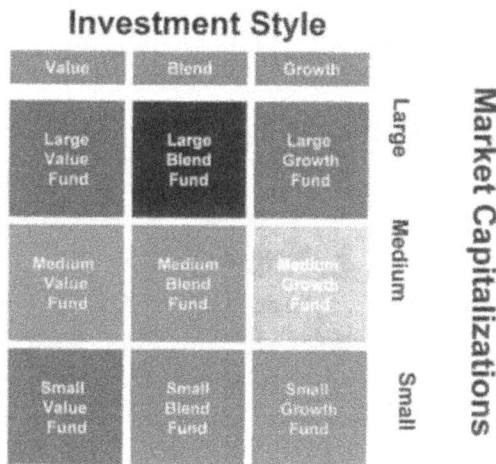

Investment Style

	Value	Blend	Growth		
	Large Value Fund	Large Blend Fund	Large Growth Fund	Large	
	Medium Value Fund	Medium Blend Fund	Medium Growth Fund	Medium	Market Capitalizations
	Small Value Fund	Small Blend Fund	Small Growth Fund	Small	

Please note that while these funds can invest in securities of companies without restriction on market capitalization, there is no guarantee that all market capitalizations will be represented in the portfolio at any given point in time.

FIG. 35: THE NINE BASKETS

When I talk about diversification, I mean don't put all your eggs in one of these baskets. The "value" block on the left-hand side are all dividend-paying companies. And then on the "growth" side, these are all capital appreciation companies. The middle block is just what is says, a "blend." And then we have the size of companies you're investing in, in terms of their capitalization. At the bottom we have the small cap companies. These are companies that have a market cap up to $2 billion. They're pretty big companies like Papa John's, BJ Wholesale, and Snapple. And then you have mid cap companies. These are between $2 billion and $10 billion, like Primerica. And then you have the large cap, the biggest companies in the world, with over $10 billion in capitalization.

Here's my mix. I want to have 1/3 of the money in "value" and 2/3 in "growth." Why do I pick that proportion? Because it mirrors the proportion of average market returns that come from dividends versus capital appreciation over the past 10 years. It's just about a 2 - 1 ratio. In terms of market cap, I want to have 15% small cap, 30% mid cap, and 55% large cap. I don't care if it's a mutual fund, a managed account, or an annuity. What I manage is not the investment, it's the philosophy. I want to make sure the mix of baskets is exactly right. A lot of investors are drawn to the largest companies because they think they're low risk. But if you don't diversify into small cap companies, you will miss out. You can see why in Figure 36.

Major asset classes versus inflation
Growth of $10,000 from 1947-2021, annual, log scale, USD thousands

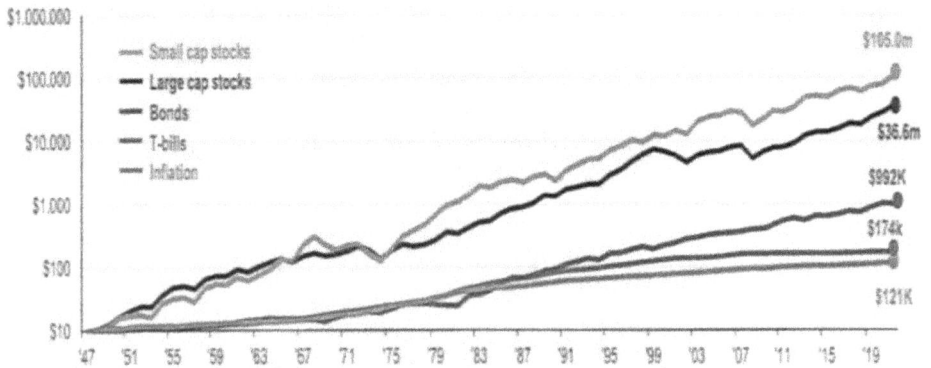

FIG. 36: MAJOR ASSET CLASSES' PERFORMANCE VS. INFLATION

If you had $10,000 invested since 1947 in only large cap stocks, your $10,000 would now be worth $36 million. Not bad! But if that $10,000 was invested only in small caps, it would be worth $105 million. So you can see why you need to have the diversification to maximize the return of the market. Why can I beat the S&P average almost every year for over 30 years? It's because I diversify through those nine baskets of equities.

In my case, I am using five different portfolio managers to achieve this asset allocation mix. Numerous parameters and variables will influence the actual mix. As I said, my target portfolio is 15-30-55, which translates to roughly 2/3 invested in growth and 1/3 in value. This is a rule of thumb, not an absolute; the ratio will never be exactly what I aim for as it depends significantly on the current economic climate. The managers need some flexibility to move up and down within a certain range to seize opportunities in the market.

In October, for example, my portfolio with that five-fund mix performed as expected. However, next month, it will likely look a little different. The reason I target 15% in small caps is that they carry the highest risk, so my goal is not only to achieve strong returns but also to justify that risk. Currently, over the last 10 years, I'm beating the S&P by 15% with a beta of 0.94, which is 6% less volatile than the market. My objective is not just to achieve great returns; it's crucial that the returns make sense in relation to the risk that you're willing to take. I'm outperforming the market by 15% while assuming 6% less risk, which is a solid position to be in.

Moreover, many investors focus solely on large-cap stocks and index funds, often neglecting small caps. While inflation isn't always a concern, lately it's been a major issue, and small-cap stocks since 1930 are the only major asset class to out perform inflation in each decade. I recommend maintaining a diversified portfolio, and as I write this book in the fall of 2024, you'll notice that small caps are beginning to make a move, particularly as we approach the presidential election. When I reassess my portfolio next month, it's likely that the small-cap allocation will increase to around 10 or 12%.

So what does this mean in practical terms? If you put away $250,000 in this portfolio for the last 10 years, you tripled your money!

Conclusion

Well, we've covered a lot. That's because there is a lot to know, and with this book you can go back and review it whenever you want to. But this is all you will ever need to know. One thing I hope I have accomplished is to dramatically lower the noise. Because a lot of what you're reading about, the hand-wringing and the panics – it's all just noise. It's irrelevant, it means nothing. You don't have to be an expert, you just have to know enough or feel comfortable enough with an advisor, that you can lower that noise level in your head, and understand that what is happening is what is supposed to happen.

Unemployment is supposed to go up, and that's exactly what's happening. Inflation is supposed to come down. That's exactly what's happening. We're right on track to have a rate decrease coming up, and you'll see a big surge in the market when that happens because people are just waiting for that. Are you prepared or are you going to wait? Are you going to say, "Well, let me see what happens?" Because, by the time it happens, you already missed it. I love it when people say to me, "Let me just give you a little money and see what you do with it. Then if it does really good, I'll give you bigger money."

Half the point of this book is so you don't make that mistake. Because while your little money made big money, your big money wasn't doing crap. And you can't go back in time. Once the opportunity is lost, it's gone. That's why if you have a time horizon of even 5 to 10 years, you've got to be a 100% in equities. If you want to maximize the return on your money you need to do that. Now, if you're older, there are things you can do in terms of putting protective wrappers on that and giving yourself some guarantees of income. But you can do that while still remaining a 100% in equities.

Our philosophy is based on building a portfolio with a 100% equity-based investment while focusing on asset class diversification, dividend income, and the protective wrappers such as variable annuities to mitigate risk and volatility. We believe this approach will help you build wealth before retirement and continue to grow your investments during retirement. Do you want to be wealthy in your retirement? Well, now you know exactly how to do it. Don't procrastinate. Let's make it happen!

To inquire about bulk book order discounts:

- Website: http://ronsphilosophy.com
- Email: ron@ronsphilosphy.com
- Telephone (610) 395-7960

Take the First Step Toward Securing Your Financial Future

At *Blue Mountain Financial Group*, our mission is simple: to help you achieve your financial goals, no matter where you are on your journey – whether you're just starting out, preparing for retirement, or already enjoying your golden years. We believe in creating personalized, sustainable financial strategies that are tailored to your unique situation and aspirations.

As part of our consultative process, we will carefully review key areas of your financial life, including:

- **Debt Solutions** – Strategies for eliminating credit card and loan debt efficiently.
- **Saving for Retirement** – Clear guidance on how much to save to ensure a comfortable retirement.
- **Education Funding** – Projections for educational costs and strategies to fund your children's future.
- **Income Needs** – Identifying income sources to secure your family's financial well-being.
- **Building Your Financial Future** – Specific steps to turn your goals into a solid action plan.

Take charge of your financial future today. Set up a free consultation with one of our experienced advisors and start building a plan that works for you. Contact us now to schedule your personalized investment review. Email: ron@ronsphilosphy.com or call (610) 395-7960. Together, we'll help you reach your financial goals!

Scan the QR Code below to sign up (in-person or online) to attend Ron's upcoming monthly seminar, *Ron's Investment Philosophy for Wealth* where he provides updated information on the market and how it impacts investers.

What Readers are Saying

"Ron Weber is the real deal—trustworthy, down-to-earth, and committed to putting your money where his and his family's is. We first met him in 2009, and though we initially hesitated due to costs, after years of solid returns, we moved our money elsewhere. That decision led to a massive loss—high fees, poor positioning, and a portfolio that shrank.

Ron had been managing our corporate and profit-sharing plans, and the returns were consistently strong—our staff couldn't believe how much better their investments performed compared to others. When we came back to Ron after our mistake, he didn't say, "I told you so." He just got to work, ran the numbers, and helped us get back on track.

If you're serious about building true generational wealth, Ron is the person you want to work with. He delivers results that last."

Dr. Ann Astolfi, - Client

"Ron Weber's book is a must-read for anyone serious about investing. We've followed his principles for years and successfully implemented them both personally and within our agency. His insights have had a tremendous impact on our organization, helping us grow our assets under management to billions. By focusing on managing the investment philosophy—rather than just the investments themselves—Ron has taught us how to make money work for us, allocate assets wisely, and balance growth with value. This book is the perfect guide for anyone looking to maximize their wealth and long-term success. We're excited to share this book with our teammates and clients, and we believe it will be a game-changer for anyone looking to build long-term financial success."

Keith Otto - Senior National Sales Director - Primerica

"I've been working with Ron for three years, and he's truly transformed my approach to investing. He's taught me how to think like the top 2% and make the most of my money. After choosing to invest with him, I've learned so much from his monthly seminars, which have given me a deeper understanding of his investment philosophy and how it can benefit me personally.

Ron is always approachable and takes the time to listen, understand my goals, and develop a personalized plan. He explains his recommendations clearly and provides reassurance during market fluctuations, making adjustments when necessary.

Ron treats his clients like family, and thanks to his guidance, I'm confident I'll be able to retire earlier than I expected. I highly recommend his new book and seminars to anyone looking to improve their financial future."

Mark Thompson – Vice President Thompson Manufacturing - Client

"I'm grateful to have worked with Ron Weber for over 23 years. When I first met him, I had a Master's degree, $1,000 in the bank, and a negative net worth. In just 90 minutes, Ron taught me more about money, investing, and business than I had learned in my entire life. His teachings on passive income and leveraging time completely transformed my financial future. Today, our net worth is in the millions, and we're on track to soon become million-dollar earners. Ron's system has changed my life, and this book is a game-changer for anyone serious about building wealth."

Pat Mullaney – Regional Vice President - Primerica